From Somalia to Snow

HOW CENTRAL MINNESOTA BECAME HOME TO SOMALIS

HUDDA IBRAHIM

BEAVER'S POND
PRESS

Copy Editor: Alicia Ester
Managing Editor: Hanna Kjeldbjerg

ISBN: 978-1-59298-778-8
Library of Congress Catalog Number: 2017904910
Printed in the United States of America
First Printing: 2017
Second Printing: 2017
21 20 19 18 17   6 5 4 3 2

Book design by Athena Currier

Beaver's Pond Press, Inc.
7108 Ohms Lane
Edina, MN 55439–2129

(952) 829-8818
www.BeaversPondPress.com
To order, visit huddaibrahim.com

From Somalia to Snow

HOW CENTRAL MINNESOTA BECAME HOME TO SOMALIS

Praise for *From Somalia to Snow: How Central Minnesota Became Home to Somalis*

From Somalia to Snow: How Central Minnesota Became Home to Somalis provides a great understanding of Somali culture, tradition, religion, and issues of integration and assimilation. In addition, it enhances awareness of the challenges and barriers that the Somali community faces. The book sheds light on the hopes, dreams, and aspirations of the Somali people. The Somali experience is similar to the experiences of other immigrant and refugee groups. They, too, want to live the American Dream. I highly recommend this book to educational institutions, the business community, health-care departments, and anyone who works and continues to build for community.

—Dave Kleis, mayor of
Saint Cloud, Minnesota

From Somalia to Snow: How Central Minnesota Became Home to Somalis is a scholarly written manuscript which is equal parts information, inspiration, and instruction. The author helps to reset a community's immigration narrative from ignorance to understanding, deficits to assets, scarcity to abundance, and fear to acceptance. In timely and important ways, this book is the collective story of *all* immigrant families who, throughout our nation's history, have shown unyielding resolve and resilience in pursuing the American Dream! A great educational tool, this book should be on the collection shelves in all school and community libraries.

—*Bruce Mohs, school board member, Saint Cloud Area Schools, Saint Cloud, Minnesota*

Hudda Ibrahim has long served as an economic adviser to our greater Saint Cloud community, to Somali and greater Saint Cloud–area businesses, and to our foreign-born residents. And now, this talented, passionate young woman has gifted our community with her much-needed and long-awaited publication filled with personal and professional insights on the journey and challenges faced by Somali immigrants and refugees that have joined our community. Thank you, Hudda, for pouring your heart and soul into writing this book, *From Somalia to Snow: How Central Minnesota Became Home to Somalis,* and for being a trailblazer, a role model, and a community leader. But most of all, thank you for being a very dear friend.

—*Patti Gartland, president, Greater Saint Cloud Development Corporation*

Hudda Ibrahim's book is a must-read because it is well researched, informative, holistic, and one of the best introductions to Somali culture for people of central Minnesota and beyond. Hudda writes with clarity, honesty, and integrity. Her very timely book is a valuable resource for the local community, for it strikes a wonderful balance between personal and professional narratives that capture critical information of her native cultural heritage.

—*Sangeeta Jhai, PhD, faculty and diversity coordinator,*
St. Cloud Technical and Community College

Hudda Ibrahim has the gift of being able to communicate across ethnic, racial, gender, economic, generational, and political barriers with a level of intimacy that requires years of cross-cultural experience. This gift illuminates the experience of the Somali community in central Minnesota and is a must-read for anyone who seeks to understand Somali American challenges as well as the challenges faced by many of our most vulnerable neighbors.

—*Lee Morgan, president,*
Morgan Family Foundation

Ibrahim's book fills a void between the scholarly literature on immigration to the United States and the practical, everyday lives of newcomers to the area as they integrate into their new communities—and as the more long-standing community members integrate to their new neighbors. If you are seeking to learn more about Somali Americans in central Minnesota, this book is an outstanding resource for learning about the history and cultural practices of Somali people. Ibrahim provides a clear pathway between Somali and central Minnesotan cultures as a knowledgeable interpreter of both groups. Her book is an excellent example of cultural translation and will be highly useful for many readers.

—*Jessica O'Reilly, assistant professor of international studies, Indiana University, Bloomington*

This book fills an important need for Saint Cloud and the surrounding area. Working from numerous personal interviews and her own life experience, Ms. Ibrahim tells the story of one of the largest communities of Somali people in the United States. It should be required reading for anyone doing any form of community work in the area and belongs on the shelves of local school and public libraries. Its value, however, is not limited to the Saint Cloud region. Anyone interested in the Somali diaspora or in refugee and immigrant populations in general will benefit from reading this account of members of one community speaking in their own voices.

—*Mark Jaede, assistant professor,*
St. Cloud State University

Ibrahim's work provides a needed examination of the complexities of Somali choices and experiences in central Minnesota. Based on numerous interviews as well as personal experiences, she clearly shows how Somali immigrant experiences are parallel and distinct from prior European immigrants to central Minnesota. Given her portrayal on individuals and locations in Saint Cloud and central Minnesota, this work is accessible for a broad audience of readers interested in humanizing the experiences of Somalis in the region and thereby debunking many problematic generalizations promoted in some segments of the media.

—*Professor Robert W. Galler,*
St. Cloud State University

This interesting and informative book explains about Somali culture, with stories of Somali resettlement and business. The writer provides a thoughtful and relevant understanding into Somali people's contemporary challenges and opportunities in central Minnesota. This book will become the key go-to resource for everyone in Minnesota or anywhere else in the United States.

—Abdi Mahad, research analyst and community education coordinator, Central Minnesota Community Empowerment Organization

Hudda's book encapsulates the cultural and religious practices of the Somali people living in central Minnesota. It also brings to the fore their unique ways of doing business as they seek to cater to the needs of their people in the growing diverse cities. It is a comprehensive, analytical, and informative book.

—Sylvester Amara Lamin, MSW, PhD, LISW, assistant professor, social work, St. Cloud State University

This important book clearly illustrates the experiences of Somalis in central Minnesota. It will be helpful and a much-needed resource for the people there. This book also offers concrete suggestions for ways by which the host community and the recently arrived Somalis can understand each other's cultures, obstacles, and achievements; foster a healthy dialogue; and build a relationship that is based on mutual respect.

—Ahmed Sheikh, Somali community elder

*To the memory of my mom, Faiza Mohammed,
schoolteacher and former politician, who introduced
me to the art of politics.*

Map of Somalia.

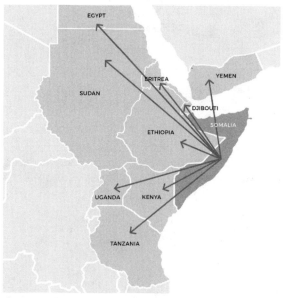

Somali people's exodus destinations during the civil war in 1991 before heading to the United States.

Contents

Chronology of
Events in Somalia

7th century: The rise of Islam in Arabia.

9th century: Islam comes to Somalia.

1860:   European colonizers partition Somalia.

1920:   Osman Yusuf Kenadid writes the first Somali alphabet (script). Before it's introduced to the public, Italian colonial authorities arrest him, and his project does not bear fruit.

1952:   Hussein Sheikh Ahmed Kaddare invents Somali orthography. Once again, the attempt to initiate a common Somali alphabet dies amid a continued struggle for independence in Somalia.

1960:   Somalia takes its independence from Great Britain and Italy. The first democratically elected government is born right after the independence.

1969: A military junta stages a coup. Siad Barre becomes the president of Somalia and rules until 1991.

1970: In October, Barre declares Somalia a socialist country and forms Somali Revolutionary Socialist Party (SRSP), known in Somali as "Xisbiga Hantiwadaaga Kacaanka Soomaaliyeed."

1972: The Somali alphabet is officially written.

1974: Somalia joins the Arab League. Arab countries give Somali students scholarships that allow Somali students to travel and study in the Gulf. The students come back to Somalia with extreme Islamic ideologies and confront Somalia's long-held moderate practice of Sufism.

1975: President Barre announces a declaration that gives Somali women equal inheritance rights. Ten Islamic scholars who oppose his equal rights decree are executed in Mogadishu by a firing squad.

1975: The Somali government forcibly nationalizes private banks, utility companies, and transportation services.

1977: Somalia invades Ethiopia to liberate Somali-led Ogaden rebels seeking secession.

1978:   The Somali government orders its troops to withdraw from Ethiopia.

1981:   The Somali National Movement (SNM) is formed in London, England.

1988:   SNM launches its first attack on the Somali army in the north.

1989:   United Somali Congress (USC), a group that wants to topple the Barre regime, is formed in Italy.

1990:   In December, an uprising to topple the government begins in Mogadishu.

1991:   On January 27, rebel groups defeat Barre's government and capture the Somali capital. Ali Mahdi Mohamed declares himself president (and serves until 1997). A power struggle begins between the armed groups who toppled Barre's regime. Millions of Somali people flee to neighboring countries to save their lives. They live in refugee camps before they arrive in the United States.

1991:   On May 18, the north of Somali, known as Somaliland, declares independence to break away from the rest of Somalia.

1998:   Puntland, central regions of Somalia, declare semi-autonomy.

2000:   On August 26, Somali clan elders elect Abdiqasim Salad Hassan, a former interior minister, as president.

2004:   Abdullahi Yusuf is elected as president.

2006:   A group of Islamists emerge and take control of Mogadishu and other parts of the country. They form the Union of Islamic Courts (UIC). Then Ethiopian troops invade Somalia to get rid of the new group. The second wave of Somali refugees flees the country to neighboring countries and then comes to the United States.

2007:   In March, African Union troops land in Mogadishu and fight the Islamist insurgents.

2009:   Sheikh Sharif Ahmed wins the presidential race.

2010   In February, the militant group al-Shabaab formally declares an alliance with al-Qaeda and doubles its suicide bombings.

2011:   In October, Kenyan troops enter Somalia for the first time to fight Islamic groups accused of kidnapping foreigners living in Kenya.

2012:   In September, members of the Somali parliament in Mogadishu elect Hassan Sheikh Mohamud president.

Now: Al-Shabaab militant groups are hunting government officials and blowing up hotels, markets, malls, and other strategic places in Somalia.

TRANSLITERATION

Throughout my book, I anglicized Somali orthography (for instance, *Abdi* instead of *Cabdi*). Anglicization of Somali names and terms are more comprehensible to Western readers. I did not transliterate names and titles quoted from other sources directly.

Foreword

WITH THIS BOOK, Ms. HUDDA IBRAHIM has provided an important service to all of us who are interested in building a strong and inclusive Saint Cloud community. There has been only one other book written about Somali members of the Saint Cloud community, *New Beginnings / Bilow Cusub*, edited by Mary Jane Berger, OSB, and published by the College of Saint Benedict in 2004. That excellent book, unfortunately out of print, focused on the lives of eleven Somalis who told their stories about their flight from Somalia and their experiences in Saint Cloud. This new book by Ms. Ibrahim, a Somali social scientist who has lived for several years in Saint Cloud, is based on more recent and extensive research (including interviews with thirty-four Somali members of the Saint Cloud community) and her own broad-based experience, including serving as a mentor to young Somali women leaders. As the first Somali to write a book about Somalis in Saint Cloud, she has important insights and understandings that only come from being a member of that community. She has given us an invaluable insider's look into the lives and culture of our Somali neighbors and some of the important challenges they face. Her thoughtful use of quotes from her interviewees lets us hear what they think in their own words and helps us to understand them better.

Ms. Ibrahim's study also is valuable because it addresses several important issues for Somalis in Saint Cloud (and elsewhere): integration and assimilation (which are not the same), the challenges facing Somali businesses and their growing role in Saint Cloud, and health-care beliefs and practices. Throughout the book, Ms. Ibrahim provides us with a good introduction to Somali culture and Islamic beliefs and the roles they play in Somalis' lives. We learn from her that like other ethnic and religious minorities, Somalis in Saint Cloud want to integrate into the broader community as they learn English, go to work and school, shop and drink tea alongside their non-Somali neighbors; they do not want to live in an isolated social enclave. But like many ethnic and religious newcomers to America, they want to hold on to important parts of their religion, culture, and identity. To many of us who have immigrant grandparents or relatives, this will sound very familiar. However, Ms. Ibrahim not only describes the various challenges facing Somalis, she also analyzes them and proposes ways to address them. I am sure readers will find her insightful.

This book is written for the general and professional audience as well as for use in the college classroom. As her former professor, a colleague, and a friend, it has always been easy for me to see that Ms. Ibrahim is a good scholar and writer, and a leader in helping us build a stronger, more inclusive community in which we all can flourish. I am sure that after reading this book, the reader will see that too.

Dr. Ron Pagnucco
Chair of the Board of Directors
Central Minnesota Community Empowerment Organization
Saint Cloud, Minnesota

Associate Professor of Peace Studies
College of Saint Benedict / Saint John's University
Saint Joseph, Minnesota

Preface

THIS BOOK IS THE PRODUCT OF MANY STORIES, experiences, and dreams. The history of Somalis in central Minnesota is new, but Somalis' stories are similar to those of the Europeans and Southeast Asians who settled in central Minnesota before them. When newcomers arrive in this country and don't know the language, they face many issues, such as getting jobs and a good education for their children, and learning how things work in their new home.

Many Americans do not understand why Somalis are here in central Minnesota, or seem to know the difference between an immigrant—who leaves his or her country voluntarily—and a refugee—who leaves his or her country under duress. Some may know that a civil war in Somalia forced people to become refugees by fleeing their homes to seek a safe environment for themselves and their families.

I have been invited to many schools, churches, and businesses to speak on Somali people's life experiences, challenges, and opportunities in central Minnesota. The idea of writing this book came to me after several of my close friends and colleagues asked me questions about Somali people and their culture. Many have wondered how thousands of Somali refugees, who have a unique culture and little knowledge of English, came to live in this cold, snowy area with people of predominantly European descent. Every day I hear many Saint Cloud–born Americans ask who these new people are. What are their lives and struggles like in Saint Cloud? Are they contributing to the Saint Cloud economy or draining resources from the community? Are they assimilating or trying to impose their culture and religion on American mainstream society?

Negative, inaccurate perceptions that Somalis are either taking away jobs or relying on welfare are a factor that encouraged me to write this book. I look into Somalis' economic contributions to central Minnesota and the challenges facing Somalis in businesses and workplaces. I wrote this book to correct some of the misperceptions about Somalis in central Minnesota.

As Dr. Ron Pagnucco mentioned in his foreword, there has not been a great deal of research published on Somalis in central Minnesota. The excellent collection of essays published in *New Beginnings / Bilow Cusub*, edited by my friend and colleague Sr. Mary Jane Berger in 2004, is out of print unfortunately. I felt it was important to collect Somali perspectives to give a portrayal of their lives today. This book is based on my own experiences and interviews with a range of Somalis in central Minnesota. For over a year, I talked to thirty-four Somalis about their experiences here.

This book is for anyone who wants to better understand the Somalis of central Minnesota and is written for a general audience as well as for high school and college students, health-care professionals, businesses, and social service agencies. It avoids technical, academic language. I hope you will discuss this book with your friends and colleagues and will try to invite some Somali friends and colleagues to join you!

Organization

This book consists of six sections. In chapter 1, I will explore major historical events, including colonization, conflict, and peace processes in Somalia, and the revival of armed groups in the north and south of Somalia. I will also look at the subsequent rise of anarchy and the root causes and trajectories of different conflict situations, which forced millions of Somali refugees out of their homeland and into refugee camps, mostly in the neighboring countries of Kenya and Ethiopia.

In chapter 2, I will discuss the history of Somali refugees and why they left their home and came to Minnesota. I will also examine secondary migration, why some Somalis moved to Saint Cloud after initially being resettled elsewhere in the United States. Immigration and refugee resettlement is not new to central Minnesota, which has seen the arrival of immigrants from Europe, Southeast Asia, Mexico, and other lands. Somalis are just one of the most recent groups to settle here.

In chapter 3, I will discuss how culture and religion influence Somalis' actions. I will also examine some of their specific cultural practices here in the Saint Cloud area.

In chapter 4, I will discuss and analyze the differences between assimilation and integration and if Somalis are assimilating or integrating into mainstream American society. I also will look at some of the factors that influence Somali integration and assimilation and what a few Somalis say about these processes.

In chapter 5, I will discuss Somali-owned businesses in Saint Cloud and its surrounding areas and the various social, cultural, and economic challenges they face.

Chapter 6 will cover Somali beliefs and practices regarding health and some of the issues in their medical care.

Participant observation, as well as personal interviews and group discussions, were used to gather information for this book. I am strongly cognizant of the fact that though I interviewed several Somalis, I cannot claim that this is a scientific study with a statistically representative sample. Nevertheless, I interviewed a range of male and female Somalis, all of whom—including elders and community leaders, business owners, health-care professionals, and young adults—have valuable knowledge and experience regarding the topics we discussed.

Some of my interviewees were born in Africa. Most of those interviewed had been in the United States from two to fifteen years, others more than twenty. I conducted my interviews in English or Somali (I am fluent in both languages). I did the English translations of the Somali interviews for this book. Most young Somalis interviewed for this book spoke fluent English; some were university graduates, undergraduates, or high school students.

Some of the older Somalis I interviewed could not speak English well, or at all. My interviews were not limited by language and the various problems such a limitation would bring.

Acknowledgments

WHILE WRITING THIS BOOK, I HAVE RECEIVED much assistance, and I am pleased to acknowledge that here. With much gratitude, I'd like to thank all the people who helped make writing this book possible.

I would like to thank Professor Ron Pagnucco, College of Saint Benedict / Saint John's University, for all his support with this book. Ron provided extensive feedback on the manuscript and guided me to other readings, articles, and research papers to understand refugees and integration better. Ron, you are an invaluable mentor, role model, and friend. I owe you a huge debt of thanks for writing the foreword that has set this book in context.

Many thanks go to Somali Americans in central Minnesota. During the process of writing this book, I interviewed thirty-four Somalis, all of whose names I cannot list here. These people were open with me. Some invited me to their homes, where we had meals together while I interviewed them. I will never forget how they agreed to share personal experiences and viewpoints. Some of them were emotional when I asked them about their life experiences during the conflict, refugee life, and the problems of adjustment in the United States.

I also want to thank Professor Sangeeta Jhai of St. Cloud Technical and Community College for her very helpful feedback. Sangeeta provided me with extensive comments on the draft manuscript.

Many friends reviewed portions of this book. I particularly want to thank Professor Jessica O'Reilly, Indiana University, Bloomington. Her suggestions and recommendations were very helpful.

I also want to thank Tess Ellens, who works at Stearns County Public Health, for reading the health chapter. She gave me some valuable information and suggestions.

I am deeply grateful to Professor Mark Jaede from St. Cloud State University, who read drafts of chapters. I know how busy he is, and I valued his suggestions greatly.

Many thanks also to Mary Belisle for her editorial work.

The following individuals offered me valuable information. Without it, I would not have been able to write this book. Among those include Mohamoud Mohamed, Saint Cloud Area Somali Salvation Organization (SASSO); Abdi Hassan; Fathiya Mohamed, refugee program supervisor at Lutheran Social Services; Abdirizak Jama, a patient care extender at St. Cloud Hospital; Tarabi Jama, executive director of Gateway; Asad Mohamed, the executive director and founder of Recover Health Resources LLC; Farhiya Idifle, a career planner at Stearns Benton Employment Training Council; Ahmed Ali, the executive director of CornerStone; Hussein Mohamud, known as Suud Olat, refugee advocate and freelance reporter; Abdi Daisane, who ran for a city council; Jama Mohamed, communication support specialist at St. Cloud Area School District 742; and many others.

Beside the names of the many Somali men and women whose personal stories are incorporated in this book, I also want to thank many Somalis who shared but asked me not to mention their names. I have chosen to protect the privacy and identity of these individuals.

I also want to thank the many people who took the time to discuss the issues of business, integration, accommodation, health, and culture.

And finally, I am indebted to Abdi Mahad, the love of my life and my greatest blessing—a writer, researcher, and community education coordinator—for his constant advice and moral support. He edited the manuscript and typed some of the chapters for me. Abdi, you surprise me with your command of the English language, your creativity, and your constant assistance. Thank you for your helpful advice, encouragement, love, and support. Many of the ideas in this book have been discussed with Abdi, and he clearly did not shy away from giving constructive criticism.

Finally, I am grateful to my editor, Alicia Ester, for helping me to put this book together. I want to thank Hanna Kjeldbjerg, who shepherded the whole project. I want to thank Athena Currier for designing this book. I also want to thank the staff of Beaver's Pond Press for believing in my work and for making the process of publishing easy. This book would not be a reality without you and your belief in me.

To each of my family members, friends, and colleagues who walked the journey of this book with me, thank you.

Chapter 1

OVERVIEW OF SOMALI HISTORY

Happy is the country which has history.

—Somali proverb

I'VE BEEN ASKED MANY TIMES where Somalia is in Africa. Somalia is in the horn of Africa and shares a border with Kenya to the south, Ethiopia to the west, Djibouti (pronounced as *jee-boo'-tee*) to the northwest, the Gulf of Aden to the north, and the Indian Ocean to the east. (See map of Somalia on page xii.)

It is difficult to explain where I'm from. Most people ask me if I am a Somalian. This reminds me of my childhood when I used to call Somali people Somalians until my dad corrected me. "There's nothing called Somalian," Dad said loudly. From that day forward, I never used that name. The term *Somali* refers to a person of Somali birth. Somalia is a country. Originally, *Somali* was derived from *Soomaal*, which means, *go and milk*. This indicates that the country was known to be generous and its people offered fresh milk to their guests. The language Somalis speak is also known as Somali. Although there are several dialects spoken in Somalia, Somali is an official language of Somalia, Djibouti, and Somali-populated regions of Kenya and Ethiopia. The Somali language was officially written in 1972. Before the arrival of the Italians and British, Somalis wrote in Arabic. English, Italian, and Arabic were the most common languages used in the media and in schools during colonialism. Besides the Islamic religion, the Somali language is the bond that holds Somali culture together.

Somalia has a population of around ten million people.[1] Nearly all Somalis are Sunni Muslim. In fact, Somalia has long been considered one of the most ethnically, linguistically, religiously, and culturally homogeneous countries in Africa.[2] There are six major clans in Somalia. Four of these are the Dir, Darod, Isaaq, and Hawiye, known as the *Samaale*, which represent about 70 percent of Somalia's population. The remaining two clans (the Digil and Rahanwein) are *Sab*, agricultural nomads representing nearly 20 percent of the population.[3] Minority clan groups comprise the remaining 10 percent of the population. Ethnic Somalis live in Somalia, Djibouti, the northeastern regions of Kenya, and the southeastern part of the Somali Regional State in Ethiopia. (See the map of Somalia on page xii.)

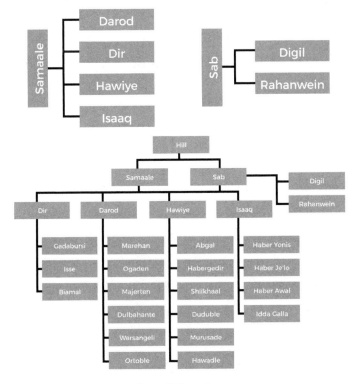

Somali clan charts.

Even though Somalia is ethnically quite homogeneous, the society is deeply divided into many rival clans and sub-clans.

For thousands of years, Somali society has followed a system of patrilineage, meaning people trace their ancestors through the male line. Not all clans are necessarily equal in terms of the number of members nor their influence or power.[4] Traditionally, clan affiliation provides members with protection and assistance. For example, based upon familial ties, politics, and ideologies, when a member of a certain clan fails to pay hospital fees, members within his or her sub-clan family get together and collect some money.

The Arrival of the Colonial Power

British, Italian, and French colonial powers competed for control of Somalia and partitioned the country into five territories: British Somaliland (north), Italian Somaliland (south), French Somaliland (northwest), Ethiopian Somaliland (the Ogaden), and Kenyan Somaliland (Northern Frontier District, NFD). The British ceded the western part of Somalia to Ethiopia and Somali-inhabited territory to Kenya.

After years of bloody struggle, the first independence youth movement emerged in 1943. When the British and Italian colonialists recognized that the Somali people were unwavering in their determination to have their own independence, the two colonial powers allowed self-rule.

By 1960, Britain and Italy granted independence to their respective territories, enabling the south and north to join as the Greater Republic of Somalia on July 1, 1960. The lands in Djibouti, Kenya, and Ethiopia, however, were not united with the north and south regions that composed the new Somalia Republic. At the time of independence, Djibouti was colonized by France, but the two territories in Ethiopia and in Kenya remained under Ethiopian and Kenyan authorities, respectively. "Somali people under the French colony voted to remain with France rather than joining the first government in 1960," one community elder said.

The Birth of the First Somali Administration

Somalia established its first democratic and civilian-led government in 1960. Siad Barre came to power in a coup on October 21, 1969. He immediately promised he would eradicate clannism and nepotism. One community elder in Saint Cloud who used to be in the Somali military said:

President Barre abolished political parties, put off the constitution, and promoted socialism. During this period, a national sense of unity was felt in

Somalia. As a whole, the nation wanted to see all Somali regions united. Somalis in the Ethiopian-controlled region of Ogaden took arms to fight against the Ethiopian government because they wanted to join with their fellow Somalis. In July 1977, heavy fighting occurred between Ethiopian troops and the Western Somali Liberation Front, a Somali ethnic Ogaden freedom-fighting movement. After the Ethiopian government launched heavy military operations, killing Somali-speaking nomadic pastoralists, the Somali army invaded and occupied much of the Ethiopian territory.

After much pressure from the international community and the direct military intervention of the Soviet Union and Cuba, the Somali army withdrew from Ethiopia. This withdrawal caused hundreds of thousands of Ethiopian Somalis to flee to Somalia. At the height of the Cold War, the Somali government cut the relationship with the Soviet Union and chose to allow the United States to open military barracks in Somalia; then WARSAW-led foreign powers intervened and took sides with Ethiopia. The Somali troops were kicked back and Ethiopia recovered its land.[5]

Very demoralized, the Somali army returned to their military barracks in Somalia. Most of the Somali troops wanted to continue the war and defeat the Ethiopian government. In the wake of the 1977–78 Somali-Ethiopian war, the two countries fell into an internal conflict, and each country funded and armed rebel movements fighting each other's governments. Ethiopia fought several secessionist movements, including the ethnic Somali Ogaden National Liberation Front (ONLF).

Meanwhile, internal unrest occurred in Somalia because of Barre's actions. In 1981, a group of exiles from the Isaaq clan in the north met in London and formed the Somali National Movement (SNM), the second armed movement ready to overthrow Barre. After the SNM formed, the Somali government committed atrocities against Isaaq intellectuals and activists believed to be sympathetic to SNM. The suppression of the Isaaq clan brought waves of protests in the north. A year after the formation of the SNM, its main leadership headquarters shifted from London to Ethiopia, where the SNM prepared for a guerrilla fight against the Barre regime. The SNM quickly captured the cities of Hargeisa and Burao in the north. Soon thereafter, the government forces regained the two cities only by using great force, including aerial and land bombardments. "The government forces responded with aerial bombing of Hargeisa, killing civilians and forcing a large number of people to flee the country," one interviewee said. "High civilian casualties and the exodus of refugees to Ethiopia further alienated the north from the Barre regime."

The United Somali Congress (USC) was established in Rome, Italy, in 1990. In December 1990, USC rebels entered Mogadishu, Somalia's capital, and heavy battle echoed throughout the city. The USC rebels and the Somali army fought for four weeks. By January 1991, the armed militiamen defeated the government forces and toppled the regime. As soon as Barre was forced out of Mogadishu, clan cleansing followed. The USC took revenge against Barre's Darod clan. The fighting continued in other regions. Both sides committed atrocities against innocent civilians.

During the conflict, thousands of Somalis fled the country to save their lives. A few moved to peaceful cities and towns in the country, with hopes that the conflict would end.

Chapter 2

IMMIGRANTS, REFUGEES, AND IDENTITIES

He who has not traveled everywhere doesn't know much.

—Somali proverb

EVERY TIME I MEET NEW FRIENDS at meetings and events, they ask me where I'm from. Oftentimes, they ask, "Are you a Somali refugee, a Somali American, or a Somali immigrant?" There has been considerable confusion in the use of the terms *immigrant*, *refugee*, and *Somali American*. It is important to describe the differences between them. Before I do so, I want to briefly recount my struggles in knowing who I was when I was a child growing up in Africa. I explain my mystifying identity in my memoir:

As soon as I was born, my family moved from one city to another. I often had trouble answering the question, "Where are you from?" We moved with Dad to different cities and towns. As an army brat, I grew up everywhere. I lived in Somalia, Ethiopia, and Kenya. In Somalia, my family lived in more than seven different places. During all those transitions, my family had a difficult time in adjusting to our new environment. The worst part of relocation was that each time we moved, I grappled with new schools with new rules. I also grappled with who I was. Was I a Somali or Ethiopian or Kenyan? On the other hand, was I a Somali-Ethiopian or a Somali-Kenyan? After quite some time, moving from one city to another became an adventure for me. In all those areas, I learned to respect people's diversity, culture, and dialects. I also learned how to be adaptable.[1]

Many people living in America are dealing with the same confusion around their identities, particularly immigrants and refugees.

An *immigrant* is a person who voluntarily moves to a foreign country to live there permanently. A *refugee* is forced to move because of conflict. Per the United Nations High Commissioner for Refugees website, "A refugee is someone who has been forced to flee his or her country because of persecution, war, or violence... [T]hey cannot return home or are afraid to do so. War, and ethnic, tribal, and religious violence are leading causes of refugees leaving their countries."[2] Throughout this book, I use the term *refugee* instead of *immigrant* to refer to first-generation Somalis who were resettled here from another country. The term *Somali American* refers to Somalis who have received their US citizenship.

Before I came to the United States in 2006, I had heard the United States referred to as "a nation of immigrants." This cliché was made popular by President John F. Kennedy in his book *A Nation of Immigrants*, written in 1958.[3] The terms *immigration* and *refugee* are not unfamiliar to the ears of most Americans. What is unfamiliar to a lot of Americans and most Minnesotans is the history, culture, and challenges of one of the state's fastest-growing refugee groups: Somalis.

The Dakota and Ojibwa Indians lived in Minnesota before European immigrants, mostly French and Scottish Canadians, began to arrive as fur traders. By 1800, settlers from New England as well as immigrants from Sweden, Norway, and Germany had settled in Minnesota, many as farmers or to work in the logging/lumber industry. A mass movement of people from Sweden to North America began in 1845 and continued until 1930[4] while "Minnesota attracted most of the approximately 850,000 Norwegians who immigrated between 1825 and 1928."[5] In 1920, 20 percent of Minnesota's total population was foreign born.[6] A wave of Southeast Asians came to Minnesota in the 1970s and '80s. At the time of the 2000 census, foreign-born residents comprised 5 percent of Minnesota's population and 11 percent of the nation's population.[7] At present, the foreign born make up 7.87 percent of the state's population. The largest and fastest-growing groups are Hispanic (Mexico), Indian (India), and Somali.[8]

History of Somali Immigration

According to D. Putman and Mohamood Cabdi, the first "Somalis came to the US in the 1920s and settled in the New York area. Most were sailors, although some worked in steel mills, and most came from northern Somalia."[9] They came to the United States to be free from colonization by various European nations. Some of those immigrants returned to Somalia when Great Britain and Italy granted independence to Somalia on July 1, 1960. Between 1985 and 1989, new conflict erupted in northern Somalia when members of the Isaaq clan tried to secede from the rest of the country. The Siad Barre regime bombarded them with heavy artillery, killing thousands of people in the north, prompting many to leave the country. Many wealthy families sent their families to the United States, most settling in New York and Washington. "These earliest Somalis who arrived in the United States in the 1980s were highly educated and possessed professional skills. Some of them were even more affluent than the rest of the community," said Abdi Mahad, a research analyst.

When civil war and Barre's overthrow erupted in 1991, thousands of refugees fleeing war and persecution sought relief in refugee camps in Kenya and Ethiopia. Some of them were eventually resettled in the United States, while others ended up in Canada, Sweden, Norway, and other refugee-receptive countries.

During the 1991 and 1992 conflict, 25,000 people died; 1.5 million people fled the country.[10] Like many European refugees during World Wars I and II, war and fear of persecution forced Somalis to leave their homes. Many of those who fled went to the neighboring countries of Kenya and Ethiopia. After a long and arduous departure from Somalia, moving from one city and town to another, my family reached Ethiopia. Like thousands of civilians, we were caught off guard. My family never thought we would go to America one day. We thought the conflict in Somalia would end and we would go back home.

The first wave of refugees was resettled in America in the 1990s. In 2006, many new refugees fled Somalia due to renewed hostilities. Between 2010 and 2015, a new wave of ethnic Somalis came over, many them from rural backgrounds in Ethiopia; most of this last group are the least educated and least skilled of the Somali refugees. New Somali refugees continue to come to the United States because of the ongoing hostilities and unrest in Somalia. In recent years, many have come to Minnesota to join their families through legal visa programs.

The Journey of Somali Refugees

When Somali refugees left their homes, they came to the neighboring countries' designated refugee camps like Kakuma, Ifo, Dadaab, and many others. Most refugees settled in the Dadaab complex of camps in Kenya. Many crossed the Red Sea into Yemen.

Hussein Mohamud lived in one of the Dadaab camps in northeastern Kenya for over twenty-one years. He said:

I was only one year old when my family fled the conflict in Somalia. All my life I knew what it was like being a refugee cloistered in a camp. I always had hopes that I would one day travel to the US and contribute to my community.[11]

Most Somalis I spoke to said that they went through a lot of problems while fleeing the civil war in Somalia. Ali Abdulle, a thirty-three-year-old man who came to Rochester, Minnesota, in 1999 and moved to Saint Cloud in 2014, said:

> A day after the civil war in 1991, my family fled the city. We ran on foot for forty miles. We boarded a bus bound for Kenya. Four days later, we were accepted as new refugees. Everywhere I looked, hundreds of refugees were boarding the truck. Most looked emaciated and famished. Some had had their family members gang-raped and butchered.[12]

According to Mariam, a twenty-nine-year-old woman:

> When the conflict began in 1991, my family ran out of Mogadishu. We left everything we had behind and hopped on a bus headed to central regions. We then hopped on a small boat to Yemen. On the boat, we were almost sixty people, very cramped in a tiny space. We had no food or water. One woman

who had a baby on the boat died. I saw an old man drinking seawater. It was chaos. Suddenly, our boat capsized. My dad carried me and my little sister. I saw older men and women drowning. Luckily, the Yemeni coast guards arrived and helped those who survived. My family could not live in Yemen because of the hatred towards refugees. We ended up living in Egypt. Somalis did not travel directly from Somalia to the United States. They went to neighboring countries. Those who had no family members or immediate relatives went to refugee settlements while others lived in cities.

Even though I was five years old, I vividly remember the day my family left Mogadishu amid the conflict.

On a Sunday morning in December 1990, I ran outside to play with my close friends. Before I finished drawing the lines of my hopscotch on the ground, I saw rebels hiding behind the walls. Some men began digging trenches. I am not sure I grasped what they were doing in my neighborhood. As I completed the last line of my hopscotch, my mom grabbed me by the neck with all her strength, her eyes wide and full of fierce determination and a mother's instinct to protect her child. I was frightened. I was disoriented. Within minutes, the city streets filled with the thunder of artillery. The men who had dug trenches fired heavy rounds that rocked our house, rattling the ceiling and sending loose plaster upon our heads. I screamed. My family huddled together like panic-stricken sheep.

As more than twelve hours went by, the fighting intensified. We could not flee for fear of getting shot or blown to pieces. By nightfall, government soldiers and rebels engaged in a pitched battle in our neighborhood. Small fires crackled like popcorn as tracer bullets lit the dark sky. Over the two-day ordeal, none of my family slept. We all lay awake on the carpet, shivering with fear. As we stayed indoors, missiles started landing around our neighborhood once again. This time debris and dust showered our rooftops. I could smell the burning houses and hear women and children screaming for help.

While preparing ourselves for a departure to a safer area, shells landed in front of our building. Terrified shouts filled in the air. The exchange of heavy gunshot and artillery fire increased in ferocity, reverberating everywhere throughout our neighborhood. We inched forward on our bellies to get to the parking lot behind our building. While we were elbow-crawling, I saw terrified people ducking behind acacia trees and concrete and brick walls as the bullets went whizzing past, falling from the sky like hail all around. We scurried into the car, my father, my mother, my brothers, and me—very startled and still shaken. Before we fastened our seat belts, my dad stepped on the gas and the car accelerated. The bullets striking the back of the car were thunderous.[13]

Before Somali refugees resettle in the United States, they go through several long screening processes involving the Department of Homeland Security, the Federal Bureau of Investigation, the State Department, the Defense Department, and the local staff at the refugee camps to verify that each refugee is no threat to national security. Because of the fear of radicalization, the number of refugees accepted by the US government for resettlement dramatically declined after the September 11 attacks. Agencies working with refugees reduced their resettlement programs to a minimum, and the vetting period for Somali refugees became three to four years, sometimes longer. The United States has resettled Somali refugees largely according to the urgency of their situations. This has significantly affected

Somalis who left their families behind. My family was told they had to go through a new interview process and new medical screening. The stringent screening process for our application meant it took more than five years for my family and me to reunite. Some other families who were about to fly to the United States caused my resettlement case to be postponed. I know some families whose security-clearance process for the United States has taken a decade. Instead of trying to move back to Somalia, they choose to continue living in countries adjacent to their homeland, such as Kenya and Ethiopia, until they are granted permanent resettlement in the United States.

After 2008, American immigration laws became more relaxed. Because of this, a significant number of new Somalis began to arrive in the United States, particularly in Saint Cloud. The bulk of the recent arrivals that I met here came from refugee camps in Ethiopia. New refugees come from four main camps: AwBarre, Kebribeyah, Sheder, and Dolow. Other new arrivals from Somalia mainly come to Saint Cloud via spouse visa.

Coming to America

United States Customs and Border Protection and United States Citizenship and Immigration Services issue an I-94 card that proves the person's legal entry into the United States. All Somali refugees coming with legal documents are given residency status and permission to work upon their arrival.

United Nations and American refugee resettlement agencies place the new arrivals in clusters in areas where the cost of living is considered low and jobs are plentiful and available, or where they already have families. Once Somali refugees arrive in Minnesota, they begin looking for jobs, and schools for their kids. When Somali refugees are resettled in Saint Cloud, they receive a one-time check from the federal government for $1,125 per person to cover basic housing and other necessities. They also are eligible for refugee benefits during the first eight months of settlement. The money and benefits are distributed by resettlement agencies, such as the Minnesota Council of Churches, Catholic Charities of Saint Paul and Minneapolis, International Institute of Minnesota, Arrive Ministries, and Lutheran Social Services Minnesota.

To understand Somali refugees' unique experiences better, let us look at some quotes from interviewees. Mariam, a college student who majored in English, said:

I will not forget my first day in the United States. I was so pleased to come here. Every morning when I woke up, I stood by the window. I said, "Where is the snow?" I questioned my parents if we came to the right destination. I was told it was summer and California did not have much snow. I spoke little English, but my schoolteachers helped me with all their ability. To learn English quickly, I had white friends at school. None of them showed me prejudice or hatred. They treated me as they treated their own. The deep feeling of a sense of belonging, support, and love helped me learn English well and be successful in school.

Somali refugees who come to the United States often exhibit ingenuity and a desire to work hard. Somalis look forward to becoming a part of, and contributors to, the American Dream. What is the American Dream for Somalis in the United States? For many, including me, it's safety, education, and equality for all.

Abdullahi, a twenty-eight-year-old man, explained:

Coming to a new country with a completely opposite way of life is a bit of a challenge. I faced a lot of problems. I dropped out of school because I could not juggle school and work. I work so hard to send half of my salaries back home. My parents live in Somalia. To pay my bills and pay my parents' bills at the same time, I work two long shifts, home-cook everything, and buy cheaper food. I've cut my monthly grocery bill in half and stopped buying expensive-brand clothes. Some nights, I sit in a dark room and think, "You departed from your homeland and came to America with dreams of a better life, but you found adjusting difficulties and poor wages." No matter how hard I work in multiple shifts, life is not a bed of roses for me. Getting a degree will help me find a good job, but I know I can't go back to school now. I am working for myself and for my family back home. If I don't work now, my family will have no other source of income. Their livelihood depends on me, and I can't abandon them now. The only way I can get out of this problem is to work hard and petition my family. If they come to the United States, I will work part-time and go to school. I am young; I will be holding on to the American Dream.

Path to Citizenship

After newcomers have resettled and stayed for a year, they can apply for a green card. The green card indicates the bearer has permanent resident status in the United States.

Green card holders may request visas for their spouses and unmarried children to live in the United States. They can go home to see their loved ones and come back within a specified time. Traveling affects the naturalization period. When the immigrant lives as a permanent resident for five years (three years for the spouses of a US citizen), he or she can apply for a naturalized citizenship. The applicant who is applying for citizenship must be older than eighteen years and pay a $595 filing fee and an $85 biometric fee, a total of $680.

In central Minnesota, a few community-based organizations assist low-income applicants. Anyone who is currently receiving public assistance, such as food stamps, Medicaid, Temporary Assistance for Needy Families (TANF), and Supplemental Security Income (SSI), can take the citizenship test without paying anything.

Once the applicant files the application, United States Citizenship and Immigration Services (USCIS) will mail a letter stating when and where the applicant's fingerprinting appointment is scheduled. (Applicants who are older than seventy-five years of age do not have to be fingerprinted.) After the fingerprinting is done, the applicant waits for interviews to be scheduled. The naturalization process takes between five and eight months, sometimes longer.

To be a citizen, the applicant must take a test on the English language and a test on US history and government (the citizenship test). The English test involves reading, writing, and speaking. For the citizenship test, each applicant is asked up to ten questions from a list of one hundred questions. To pass the test, one must answer at least six questions correctly. If the applicant fails, he or she can retake the test between sixty and ninety days from the date of the first test unless the applicant qualifies for an exemption. For older Somali applicants, passing the citizenship test is a common problem. "The older people get, the harder it can be to memorize one hundred questions," said Abdi Mahad. "I see many failing the test. Those who do not pass a second time give up becoming a naturalized citizen because they do not want to begin the application process over. They renew their green cards instead. Studying materials for the citizenship test is not that easy for older Somalis."[14] Per United States Citizenship and Immigration Services, the pass rate among all applicants for naturalization nationwide is 91 percent as of 2016.[15]

Older people who suffer memory loss may have their family doctor write a waiver letter stating their health problems. Therefore, these applicants will obtain their citizenship without the test and English language requirements.

Applicants who do not possess a knowledge and understanding of US history and government may take classes. There are many community and nonprofit organizations in Saint Cloud that offer citizenship and English as a Second Language (ESL) courses. Hands Across the World is among those organizations in the Saint Cloud area assisting recent immigrants and refugees in speaking English and studying the materials for the citizenship test.

Somalis are aware of the benefits of becoming a citizen: voting rights, citizenship for children born abroad, and travel back home with a US passport for a lengthy time. Most federal jobs and running for office requires citizenship. Most Somalis strive to be citizens to petition their families to join them in the United States more swiftly. Mohamed Abdullahi, a father whose children live in Africa, talked about the importance of being a US citizen:

> Even though I live in Saint Cloud, I travel back home twice a year to see my wife and children who were all born in Africa. If I did not have an American passport, my children would not have been American citizens. Some of my coworkers often ask me, "Can your child become a citizen if your child is born abroad?" Yes, a child born abroad to one US citizen parent and one alien parent acquires US citizenship at birth.[16]

Why Minnesota?

When I was in Africa, I used to hear members of my family in Minnesota saying the state was freezing cold, but Minnesotans were welcoming and friendly. I saw Somalis who had "Minnesota fever." Somalis continue to gravitate toward Minnesota more than anywhere else in the United States, often because Minnesota has one of the largest Somali populations in the country. Somalis can open businesses to sell ethnic clothing and food that reminds them of home. When asked why Minnesota, a Somali named Shamhad said, "Being in Minnesota reminds me of living in Somalia except the weather."

While living in a refugee camp in northeastern Kenya for over twenty-one years, Hussein Mohamud heard many good things about Minnesota:

> All those years, I heard many families in the refugee settlements praying to get resettled in Minnesota. We heard that Somalis established a tightly knit community. America is referred to as a "land of opportunity" where refugees believe in liberty, equality, hard work, and prosperity; many Somali refugees in the refugee camps believe Minnesota is the land of opportunity. For many, the term

Minnesota is synonymous with America. Many of us had already planned to go to Minnesota even if we were taken to different states. We always knew the cities where Somali communities were dispersed; services earmarked for new immigrants, such as hospital interpretation, might not be culturally or linguistically compatible elsewhere.[17]

For decades, Minnesota has been a favorable destination for immigrants coming to the United States. Unlike Somalis, Scandinavians and Germans moved to Minnesota because the climate was much like their homeland, as was the soil for farming. Somalis hail from an arid land on the horn of Africa. They practice the Islamic religion. Many may wonder why thousands of Somalis, who have a unique culture and little knowledge of English, choose to live in this cold and snowy state.

In the 1990s, new Somali arrivals had no choice of where to go for their resettlement. Many new Somali refugees flooded into Minnesota because refugee resettlement agencies here became exceptionally active and worked in close cooperation with the US government to resettle many refugees in Minnesota. Those agencies play the biggest role in deciding where refugees go first. Minnesota's many active resettlement providers help new Somalis with temporary cash assistance, employment, housing, low-cost legal services, ESL classes, community development programs, and other outreach services.

"The Somali refugees did not flock to Minnesota on their own in the 1990s," said Abdi Mahad. "As soon as they were brought to Minnesota, they formed a cohesive network and established businesses. Their extended families joined them. Even today, new immigrant families travel to Minnesota because they have some immediate relatives and kin connection.[18] Somalis who have been resettled in Minnesota often spread the news of Minnesota's best hospitality. Then every one of us starts thinking, 'Now we know where we will be going.'"[19] While interviewing people for my book, I grasped that Minnesota still is one of the favorite destinations for Somalis.

Why Did Somalis Come to Saint Cloud?

In rural Somalia, pastoral nomads migrate in search of better pastures and water for their livestock. Before any movement begins, young scouts go out to distant places to look for areas where rainwater and pastures are abundant. These pathfinders return to share whether the locations they have visited are habitable or not. This type of exploration is known in Somali as a *Sahan*. Similarly, Somali refugees in America often travel around in search of places that offer plenty of job opportunities, good education, affordable housing, and a safe environment. Like itinerant pastoral nomads in Somalia, Somali refugees in America do not stay in one place for long. They are constantly on the move in search of better places to live. "Even if they have family in Saint Cloud," said Abdi Mahad, "Somalis will move elsewhere in search of work, if necessary." A popular Somali proverb says, "*Sahan la'aan inuu guuraana waa gardarro,*" which literally means, *Moving without exploring is wrong.* Abdi Hassan, a professional behavioral specialist, was among the first group of Somali people who arrived in Saint Cloud. He explains how Somalis got here:

> Migration to central Minnesota happened in three distinct phases. We were only ten men and two girls who chose to come to Saint Cloud from Minneapolis in 1999. Most Somali people came to the area in 2000 and 2001 from Marshall and Rochester when the plants where they were working were closed. The first wave consisted only of unmarried Somalis, mostly young and middle aged. We found jobs at Electrolux, Jennie-O, Gold'n Plump, and many other businesses in the area. Our numbers rose quickly. We started renting

apartment buildings and lived together to save our money. We shared food and renting cost. We even shared cars. The arrival of many single men created a high demand for Somali-owned restaurants, tea shops, grocery and clothing stores. Soon after that, small-scale businesses increased. As the first group of Somalis settled in and made a buck, news spread through word of mouth. More Somalis joined them. Between 2002 and 2004, a second wave of Somalis, mostly married families, arrived from other cities in Minnesota and other states. These families saw an opportunity to improve their lives and those of their children. They found jobs in manufacturing, construction, food service, and meat-packing as their kids went to school.

As the community grew larger, the demand for taxi and truck driving was on the rise. Many young men took jobs in fishing industries in Alaska while many others worked as taxi and truck drivers. Those newcomers in turn invited their relatives in other states to join them in the meat-packing industries that required no prior language skills and education. The third influx of Somalis who had no English skills and edu-cation came between 2010 and 2015 to central

Minnesota from Ethiopian refugee camps. The notion of inviting your loved ones and friends to the new working opportunity is not unique to the Somali people.[20]

As the Somali community grew and their businesses flourished in Saint Cloud, they established nonprofit organizations and agencies to assist newer Somalis in navigating their new home. These organizations provide resources to the Somali communities in housing, transportation, interpretation, employment, mentoring, and tutoring. Mohamoud Mohamed, executive director of the Saint Cloud Area Somali Salvation Organization (SASSO), who has been assisting Somali refugees for over fifteen years, agreed with Abdi Hassan about how Somalis came to Saint Cloud. "The greatest surge of Somali secondary immigrants came in the wake of a small group of young men who arrived in Saint Cloud in 1999. When they returned to their cities and states, they spread the word of multiple working opportunities in meat-processing plants."[21]

Somalis, like the Europeans and Southeast Asians who came before them, gravitated toward Saint Cloud because, according to *IQ* magazine, "Saint Cloud has been a warm and welcoming place for Somali families. Government, church, and nonprofit leaders seem to remember the stories of their own immigrant ancestors and find it in their hearts to help."[22] Many Somali newcomers chose resettlement in the Saint Cloud area because they could easily find work that did not require advanced English language skills. They also looked for a city where they could afford to live and raise families. Some interviewees told me they were among the first Somalis who moved from Marshall, Minnesota, to Saint Cloud when Marshall's Heartland Poultry plant was closed in 2003.[23]

Somalis have changed the demographic composition of the city, previously a predominantly white town. In fact, Somalis are one of the fastest-growing minority groups in the Saint Cloud metro area today. "Somalis in Saint Cloud represent a cross-section of Somali society and regions, and even though there is not a precise statistic for this," said Abdi Mahad, "the majority of recent Somalis came from Ethiopia and Kenya, while perhaps 20 percent arrived from Somalia and the rest from Egypt, Yemen, and the Gulf." According to the Minnesota Department of Human Services, more than 1,564 Somali refugees were brought to Stearns County between 2003 and 2015.[24] It still is difficult to determine the exact number of Somalis who call Saint Cloud home. Official estimates range from six thousand to well over ten thousand people.

Mohamoud Mohamed noted that the Somali population in the 2000s was about forty families. "People who came to Saint Cloud initially contacted their relatives in other cities in Minnesota or in other states or back home about the working opportunities in their new city. They also told them that they found jobs that did not require them to speak much English. Their family, relatives, and friends then followed the early arrivals. Soon you had a litany of Somali newcomers who were new to the city. Each year, the Somali population grew as they established many tightly knit communities in the south of Saint Cloud because they did not want to lose touch with their national roots. Between 2000 and 2009, most Somali refugees settled first in the La Cruz neighborhood area, but later, they moved to the north, and now are widely distributed throughout Saint Cloud and its environs."[25]

Secondary Migration

Secondary immigrants are people who were settled first in one state or city and then decided to move to another place because of better opportunities. Somalis often ask of a new place, "Are there many Somalis there? Do they have mosques and religious studies centers? Do they have halal grocery stores? Do they have better opportunities for jobs and schooling?"

Mohamoud estimated that approximately 80 percent of newcomers are secondary migrants in Saint Cloud.

In the number of interviews I conducted in the Saint Cloud Somali community between October 2015 and March 2016, I found that the most significant determinants of Somalis' secondary migration were socioeconomic factors, community resources, access to the job market, housing availability, educational opportunities, and the presence of family and clan family groups. "Between 2000 and 2005, the large population drawn to settle in Saint Cloud was of secondary immigrants who were laid off from meat-processing plants in Marshall," said Mohamoud. "Today, some new arrivals come to central Minnesota because of their family members sponsoring them from Africa."[26] Jama Alimad, a local Somali community elder, moved from San Diego to Saint Paul. After a brief stay in Saint Paul, he asked around about a good city to raise his family. He then moved to Saint Cloud in 2004.

In Search of Economic Opportunities

Somalis move from one place to another to search for jobs. Most migrate to areas where working opportunities are greater. This is one of the major reasons Somalis come to Saint Cloud.

One of my interviewees told me he moved to Saint Cloud from California three years ago. "There is a plenty of work in the urban job market in California. Most of those jobs are related to high tech. Since my English language proficiency is limited, I chose to move to this small city." Six out of ten new arrivals that I met during my interviews said the search for economic opportunities brought them to settle in Saint Cloud. Will Somalis who have flocked to the Saint Cloud area in such large numbers stay in this city? The answer to that question depends on the constant availability of jobs in industries that do not require advanced English language skills.

Abdi Hassan, who was among the first Somalis who came to the Saint Cloud area, explained:

> In the 2000s, factory-related jobs were plentiful and employers wanted to hire more people. Some employers regarded Somalis' movement as a blessing. Meat- and poultry-processing plants have become a major hirer of Somalis in the region for over a decade. As the Somali population has grown, the availability of jobs has become very scarce. Some Somalis have moved back to Alaska. Many others are now truck drivers who shuttle throughout the States.[27]

For over a decade, Somalis worked at these plants. Today, some Somalis are leaving the city due to lack of jobs. "When

I was laid off in 2013," said one of my interviewees, "I drove to Moorhead and Fargo to look for a job. I stayed there for five days until I found a job. Before I allowed my family to join me, I rented an apartment, and then they moved in with me a month after." Some of my interviewees who graduated from local colleges and universities informed me that Saint Cloud is losing many talented young Somali professionals because they can't find professional jobs. A small number do find jobs; however, they are overqualified and underpaid.

Housing

Somalis with larger families struggle to find safe and well-maintained housing in the United States. Most people I interviewed said that they moved to the Saint Cloud area looking for affordable housing options.

Many Somalis come to Saint Cloud with their extended families, with some family units consisting of more than ten people. Finding an apartment that will house them all is quite challenging. Many extended families have diffi-culty finding affordable rental housing that is publicly sub-sidized. One major problem I always see is the availability and accessibility of private housing for low-income Somali Americans. For example, in 2012, a family of fourteen moved to Saint Cloud from Minneapolis. After searching for a six-bedroom apartment for over a month, they chose to rent two apartments that each cost $550 a month.

A mother of ten, Asho Ali complained about the strictly enforced occupancy limit that splits her family into two. "Now my own family members live in two apartment buildings that are located within walking distance of each other. In Somalia, we all live under one roof." Many families like Asho's have difficulty in finding a large enough apartment that can house a large family. Because American families do not live with their extended family members, this type of housing is not in demand.

"Some extended family members rent apartments next to each other so they can live close to one another," said Mohamud Mohamed, the SASSO executive director. "Because of refugee family size, those families need five- or six-bedroom affordable housing, which can be rare here in Saint Cloud." New refugees who move from other cities often face more hardships than ever. When these secondary migrants arrive in Saint Cloud, they stay with their relatives, friends, or distant kinfolk. For example, before Asho found two apartments for her family, her friend welcomed her and her kids to live in the friend's apartment. "I came here with my five kids here in Saint Cloud. Because of my limited English skills and me having no car, I had difficulty in looking for an apartment building and navigating through the complex rental paperwork. During my search for an apartment, I slept in my friend's living room for over three months," she complained.

It is worrisome that people uprooted and displaced by conflict in Somalia once again face homelessness in America. Many Somalis new to central Minnesota, mostly secondary migrants, share rooms with relatives who came here before them. Many more families are struggling to pay their rent and utilities or for basic household items. Some choose to rent one bedroom and cram themselves into it. However, this can be a problem for the property owner, who must comply with occupancy guidelines mandated by city or federal regulations.

A woman who moved from Washington, DC, to the Saint Cloud area in 2008 with her ten children said she was told that most devout Christian white families in central Minnesota had too many children, so finding a big apartment fitting her kids would not be problematic. "I met way too many Somali families like mine who were duped into believing that immigrants with large or extended families could find five to six bedrooms accommodating all of their family members."

Abdirahman Nur, a newcomer, said:

I have met some families who were turned away because they have many children. Some do not know what to do and who to reach for a complaint. Some newcomers face housing discrimination, but they feel powerless to confront due to language and cultural barriers. Each month, the housing office notifies us to add ten to twenty dollars at the top of each month's rent fee. When we ask them about rent increases without a prior notice, no one gives us a satisfactory answer. I know the property owners are taking advantage of their Somali tenants who are new to the country. The property owners know we are not that familiar with the US fair housing laws. Sometimes when air conditioners or stoves stop functioning, we call the office to notify the problem, but they do not come to us in time to fix them. Many of us assumed that property owners wanted to push us out.[28]

While landlords attempting to take advantage of their tenants is nothing new, language barriers cause extra problems for understanding the American rental system. Because of such barriers, some recently arrived Somali tenants sign paperwork without understanding the content of the agreements. Abdullahi arrived with six of his kids from Ohio. One day, the rental office notified him that he would need to move out in a week. After a confused look, he called his friend for an interpretation. Sadly, Abdullahi had signed a one-year lease only, but he had no idea that he had done so.

Mohamed said that his organization assists cosigning rental contracts for hundreds of Somali families new to the culture of the country:

> When the new arrivals are looking for property to rent, they face a lot of challenges. Apart from the apparent language barriers, the new refugees do not have any prior rental and employment history. Our organization is aware of the fact that when we cosign, we take financial responsibilities of renting that apartment. We assist new arrivals in finding jobs, so they pay the rent on time.[29]

Besides SASSO's programs to assist new arrivals, there are many organizations and agencies in the Saint Cloud area that play an active role in helping Somali newcomers overcome housing and employment barriers.

Religious Schools

My interviewees told me they came to Saint Cloud because of the growing number of religious institutions that cater to the Somali community. Some Somalis move to Saint Cloud just because of the mosques that offer after-school Islamic teaching programs. For example, Ali Abdi's family moved from Mayfield, Kentucky, in 2013 largely because of the existence of a mosque in the city. "Finding a place of worship was no easy task for us," said Ali.[30] The availability of

Hussein Mohamud is a twenty-five-year-old Somali who came to the United States in 2013. He lived in Tennessee before settling in St. Cloud in April 2015. He united his family in St. Cloud. He is currently working as an interpreter at the Bridge-World Language Center.

"Apart from reuniting with my family, I came here for several reasons. Most of my close friends from back in Africa live in Minnesota. I also moved here just because I wanted to be a part of the vibrant and growing Somali community."

Islamic schools has also been a strong incentive for Somalis to move to the city of Saint Cloud. Halima Ali, a mother of six, moved from Marshall, Minnesota, in April 2011. She said she did not find a good Islamic school for her young children in Marshall and was afraid that her children would be negatively influenced by their peers in the public school. A week after her arrival in Saint Cloud, she enrolled her children in an Islamic school at the mosque.

Family Reunion

Naturalized citizens and permanent residents who have family members living outside of the United States can file petitions to reunite with loved ones. Family reunification is another reason new refugees from Africa arrive in Saint Cloud. Rahma Abdi, a nineteen-year-old college student, came directly to Saint Cloud on a visa from Africa in 2013 after her dad petitioned for her. Her dad has been living in central Minnesota since 2005. Somali American parents can file for their kids who live outside the United States to join them.

Ummu Abdi, a twenty-two-year-old student, arrived in Saint Cloud in 2014 from a Kenyan refugee camp. Before she could resettle in the United States, she notified the refugee resettlement agency and the United Nations that she had an aunt in Saint Cloud. "I flew from Nairobi, Kenya, to Minnesota," said Ummu. "If I had not had any relative in Saint Cloud, the UN could have referred me to any other country or city." Traditionally, Somalis tend to congregate in communities where they have families and immediate or distant relatives.

Fathiya Mohamed joined her uncle in Saint Cloud when he called her to help him set up his restaurant. She finally decided to settle in Saint Cloud when the business became successful. Fathiya went to St. Cloud State University and interned at Lutheran Social Service (LSS). Today, she is a refugee program supervisor at LSS, where she assists newcomers in settling down.

I also came to Saint Cloud to join my brothers. If my family members had not been in Saint Cloud, I would not have come here initially.

Robust Refugee Resettlement Agencies

Saint Cloud refugee resettlement programs are very active. This strong refugee support network lures Somalis from Africa who want to join their families now residing in central Minnesota. Asho Mohamed, a mother of four, came to Saint Cloud from Denver in early 2006. She sponsored her spouse's resettlement and waited for more than four years for action. The refugee resettlement agencies in Denver did not help her reunite with her husband. Because of the complexity of resettlement there, she chose to move to Saint Cloud, where she thinks the refugee resettlement agencies are more successful than any other area in the United States today. Hundreds of other Somali families like Asho's have made their home here because they are also in the process of bringing their loved ones to America.

According to Fathiya Mohamed, "The agency resettles 215 individuals per year."[31] Fathiya explained that LSS assists with the resettlement of the newly arrived in Saint Cloud, and their services consist of reception and placement, dealing with resettlement, refugee employment services, and refugee social services. Fathiya stresses, "Refugee social services often deals with secondary arrivals, helping refugees with housing, school enrollment, employment, community referrals, and various other necessities that would make their relocation stress-free."[32]

New Arrivals

A few refugees arrive directly from Africa without having family ties to Saint Cloud. Once they are brought here, they receive assistance from their fellow Somali residents.

Oftentimes, newcomers find a strong support network from their community. They feel more at home near others who belong to their same clan. In general, refugees who come from the same clan usually stay together.

Clan and Relatives

Two weeks after the United States resettled him in Arizona, Mohamed Ismael decided to move to Saint Cloud. He knew his clansmen lived predominantly in the Saint Cloud area:

> When I was laid off, I had no close family members and relatives around me. My neighbors advised me to go to Minnesota, where Somalis have a strong network. I stayed in Minneapolis for a few weeks until I moved to Saint Cloud. One of my close relatives took me to his home and asked me to share a room with his son. I lived in his home until I could fend for myself.[33]

Somali people use clan allegiances for both positive and negative means. Traditionally, clan membership offers members insurance. Occasionally, some use it to discriminate against each other. Most Somalis in the United States help one another. A few new arrivals may move to areas or neighborhoods that their clan family groups reside in, because they need friends and relatives to help them resettle and navigate the system.

A Somali man who prefers to remain anonymous said, "When I arrived here in Saint Cloud, I certainly felt welcome. This has been my only home since then. I spoke no English and had no idea what to expect, but I knew many distant relatives whom we grew up with in Ethiopia."

Nejah Ibrahim, a twenty-one-year-old college student, told me his family moved from Alaska to Saint Cloud in 2013. "My mom knew some of our relatives and friends living in Saint Cloud. As soon as we arrived, our relatives welcomed us and gave us a place to stay until we found our own apartment," said Nejah. "In Saint Cloud, Somalis interact with one another. Neighbors exchange visits. We go to their houses, and they come to ours. We share a meal together, study together, and play sports together, unlike members of the Somali community in Alaska, who isolate themselves with their work and school. In Saint Cloud, my family felt home."[34]

Abdi Hassan notes that the first Somali influx clustered in the city was united. Abdi explained his experience:

Regardless of clan affiliations, we were all one community. We all shared rooms, food, and cars together. We welcomed new Somalis, gave them a place to sleep, gave them money, and helped them get jobs. We did all just because we knew what it was like struggling in a new country, where everything was new to them. I know many late-arriving Somalis who came to Saint Cloud for the first time were terrified. Many of them could not speak English. No matter what their experiences were, we were here to welcome them, treat them like our family members, and help them navigate their new home.[35]

Mohammed Abdi, who moved with his family to Saint Cloud in 2014, said:

I moved to Saint Cloud's tight-knit Somali community for one reason: I wanted my clansmen to assist me with adjusting to the challenges of living in a new environment. No newcomers will be able to navigate American life without any support from their own community. When you are new to a place, you don't speak English, and you don't have genuine community support, your transition will be ineffective. You feel like you are thrown out of a plane with a parachute into a desert. You have no water, food, or home. All you do is wander around, not knowing to which direction you are heading. You feel lost and confused. You feel weak and vulnerable. However, when you have immediate relatives who are willing to support and mentor you, you know what to do. Somali community mentors continue to voluntarily help newcomers learn some conversational English, how to drive, open a bank account, find a job, and get the government benefits they qualify for.[36]

Education

The presence of colleges and universities, particularly St. Cloud Technical and Community College, St. Cloud State University, and the College of Saint Benedict / Saint John's University, has a positive influence in central Minnesota. Somali parents make the decision to move to Saint Cloud so their children can benefit from a superior education and plentiful job opportunities. However, even though the desire to go to college is high among members of the Somali community, they face many challenges that hinder them from enrolling in those institutions of higher learning.

Challenges New Somali Refugees Face in Central Minnesota

When I came to America in 2006, everything I saw for the first weeks was new to me. I even avoided eating because the food tasted different from what I was accustomed to. Every time my brother went off to work at T-Mobile, I stayed home because I knew no one in the city. I felt isolated. Some days, I took a chair, sat by the window, and just watched the world go by.

Many Somali refugees have felt the same. I see that almost all the refugees arriving in Saint Cloud find themselves immediately faced with new difficulties and challenges: Where will we live and raise a family? How will we find jobs? How will we pay the bills? How long will it take to learn English? How do we enroll our children in public school? When will we sponsor the rest of our family from Africa?

New arrivals with English language proficiency find more opportunities in metropolitan areas. Some must migrate to other areas offering more plentiful job opportunities. Most refugees take the first job that becomes available to them.

One of the most noticeable barriers new arrivals experience is the English language and the American culture. Somali refugees enter an environment very different from the one they left behind. The language barrier often hampers refugees' efforts to communicate, find a job, and navigate through a new system. In Saint Cloud, many meat-processing plants and warehouses that once hired Somalis regardless of their language skills no longer hire refugees with limited English. New arrivals with no or limited English proficiency often have a difficult time accessing medical services, transportation, emergency and food assistance, educational resources, and more.

Somali families come to Saint Cloud to make better lives for themselves and their families, but many face troubles and tribulations that seem worse than those they left behind. Some challenges make new arrivals regret moving to a new location. Mohammed Abdi told me he'd had difficulty finding a job since he came to Saint Cloud. "I will be very glad if the resettlement agency that brought me to the US would take me back home. In Africa, I never worried about finding a job and failing to put a roof over my family's head. I used to work hard. Today, I am struggling to find work." When meeting with him, I detected the frustration he went through. Apart from unemployment, he faced transportation problems and a language barrier. Many arrivals like Mohamud face some daunting challenges each day, though many of us are not fully aware of their problems.

On top of all the new challenges Somali refugees face here in Saint Cloud, many may be suffering from post-traumatic stress stemming from the horrifying experiences they suffered in their home countries of Somalia, Kenya, and Ethiopia. Some saw violence, carnage, and even watched family members be killed and gang-raped in front of their eyes. Some women who experienced sexual violence and rape while fleeing Somalia avoid seeking medical assistance here because of the social taboo within the Somali community. Such a cultural taboo generates an extra hurdle for Somali women. However, the very refugees who have witnessed gruesome massacre, torture, and other violent acts today are victims of overt and subtle discrimination, Islamophobia, and mistreatment in the workplace, including bullying, physical intimidation, harassment, and verbal insults.

The Possibility of Going Home

Not all Somali Americans are planning to stay in central Minnesota for the rest of their lives. Somali senior citizens prefer to be in Somalia largely because of Minnesota's cold and snow. Some families have moved back there because they want to raise their families in their own culture. Some college graduates have better-paying job opportunities in Somalia. Thus far, those Somali Americans who have returned to Somalia mostly work in the government or for humanitarian agencies. Some have run for political office. Some Somalis I interviewed said that they did not intend to go back to Somalia. Those who want to remain in the United States have a dilemma as to whether to integrate or assimilate into their new country.

Chapter 3

CULTURE AND RELIGION

A community becomes extinct when its language and customs become extinct.

—Somali proverb

WHEN I NAVIGATE THE NARROW AISLES of Saint Cloud's Somali-owned shopping malls, I see brightly colored women's dresses jutting out of clothing stores and smell the pleasant aroma of cardamom-raisin basmati rice coming from restaurants. The mall is usually bustling as many Somali customers buy food, ethnic essential oils, Somali music CDs, henna dye, books written in Somali, and

Somali-made crafts. Every time I go to the Somali stores, I am filled with nostalgia for my childhood days. I am reminded of the picture of my parents holding my hand as we move through the narrow maze of Bakara Market, the biggest mall in Mogadishu. Somalis, no matter where they go in the world, are much attached to their roots. Eateries and food markets often provide Somalis with a culinary connection to our homeland. How do Somalis retain their customs and values in Saint Cloud beyond the market, restaurants, and mosque?

Somali People in Saint Cloud

Like other newcomers before them, Somalis bring their faith, language, clothing, music, folk dances, ethnic foods, cultural practices, and identities with them. Their unique cultural characteristics add to the diversity of the communities they settle into.

Somali culture is a combination of African and Arab influences. Even though Somali people are culturally, linguistically, and religiously homogeneous, the regions in which they are born and raised influence their culture. For example, Somalis in Saint Cloud do not only speak Somali; they also speak Amharic (from Ethiopia), Kiswahili (from Kenya), and Arabic (from Yemen and elsewhere). Coming from such diverse regions, Somalis may have some differences in culture and cuisine.

Etiquette and Customs

Somali people, no matter where they live, strongly cling to some elements of their culture because they consider them essential to their lives and future. Here are some of the more common points of etiquette and customs distinctive to Somalis.

Food Etiquette

Food is an important component of the Somalis' cultural identity. Families come together to share meals. I am often asked, "What types of food do Somalis eat? Are Somalis vegetarian? What kind of diet do they have? Do they have etiquette regarding food and eating?"

Factors like religion, culture, social status, and geography influence Somali food etiquette. Of foremost importance is *halal*. In Arabic, the term means things permissible to use or perform that do not go against *Sharia*, Islamic law, based on the teaching of the Quran and the *Hadith*, which are the recorded teachings and practices of the Prophet Mohammed. Most Somalis follow Islamic law, which prohibits the consumption of pork or derivatives, alcohol, other intoxicating beverages, and drugs. For example, Somalis eat halal meat that comes from animals slaughtered according to Islamic dietary law, similar to Jewish kosher regulations. In Islam, the manner of slaughtering must prevent any unnecessary suffering to the animal. As the animal is slaughtered, the phrase *"Bismillahi rahmani rahim"* (which literally means, *In the name of God, the Most Gracious, and the Most Merciful*) must be loudly articulated. This phrase has great significance in Islam because it is recited before each chapter of the Quran. If the phrase is not read during slaughtering, the meat will be deemed "impure."

In Somali custom, the use of spoons and forks is an alien practice exported to Somalia from the West. It is disrespectful to refuse food or tea offered to you when visiting a Somali home. For your host to avoid embarrassment, he or she provides you with a large meal. People eat with their right hand because they use the left hand for personal hygiene. Also, when you want to serve food or drink to a Somali person, you give them the food with the right hand. My parents disciplined me to not use the left hand as a child, so I began to consider the left hand unclean. This right-hand preference, in part, can be linked to the Islamic faith. Leaving a bit of food on the plate indicates that the host has offered you more than enough food. When Somalis come to your home, they accept your food even if they are not hungry because they do not want you to feel offended. Food is always shared from a single plate in the middle of the table without the use of knives and forks. Culturally, Somalis in America often offer to help the host with food preparation, clearing up after a meal, and washing dishes.

In many Somali households, you will find that people sit on a floor mat to eat their meals. Americans may find this awkward because they are used to sitting on chairs.

There is a correlation between consumption of certain parts of food and social status in the Somali community. For example, most clans have a cultural and tribal taboo against the consumption of domesticated animals' internal organs. Those who eat entrails, such as brains, tongues, hearts, or intestines are thought to be from minority clans. The major clans of Somalia still hold food prohibitions. Most believe entrails of butchered animals are unfit for human consumption. Many others may argue that the ingestion of viscera will dwindle their nobility and clan status.

Somali cuisine has regional variations. Somalis from the northern and central regions of Somalia eat plenty of meat, whereas eating vegetables and fish are common in the coastal towns and cities in the south of the country. In the southern part of the country, thanks to the influence of Italian cuisine, people tend to eat more pasta than rice. Also in the south, the banana is an important part of the diet; traditionally, the banana is eaten with every meal. For Somalis from southwestern regions, such as Middle and Lower Shebelle, ground sorghum is served with plantains as a major food staple. Moreover, ethnic Somalis who live in the Ethiopian-controlled territories eat *injera*, an Ethiopian tangy and spongy flatbread, and those Somalis born and raised in Kenya prefer *ugali* (a dish made of cornmeal) with collard greens, known as a *Sukuma wiki* in Swahili.

Pastoral nomads live solely on dairy products, meat, and grain. A traditional dish known in Somali as *soor*, which is corn grits served with milk, is also common among Somali pastoral nomads. Somali diets have been influenced by Indian foods, such as chapatti, basmati and biryani rice, and samosas, which are deep-fried triangular-shaped dumplings or pastries, usually filled with spiced ground meat, fish, or vegetables. In addition, the ingredients brought by Arab traders still heavily influence Somali cuisine as they have for centuries. For example, the Arabs introduced spices, such as nutmeg, cumin seeds, tamarind, saffron, turmeric, cinnamon, ginger, and cloves to Somalia.

Celebrating over a Big Meal

In the Somali culture, people eat for solidarity and togetherness as well as for physical nourishment. Many

Somalis I interviewed said that eating from the same plate signified a sense of unity and sharing of available resources.

I grew up in a household where my family sat around the table to eat from one big plate. I often saw my mom inviting her friends over for a meal. My dad and grandpa would come home with their friends at mealtime as well. At the lunch table, we all talked over food. My mom and dad made time in their busy schedules to cook for our family. I still recall how all my brothers and sisters helped Mom get ready. We all discussed how our days had gone and talked about matters that concerned all of us.

As soon as my mom died in 1998, my brothers, sisters, and I went in different directions. Even though all of us live in America, we have not all shared a meal since. Today, I miss such food gatherings, and the food I eat does not taste the same. Every time I try to get my family to come together at mealtime, only one or two show up because of their busy schedules. My grandpa taught me a bit of wisdom: "A family's relationship grows when they take food from the same dish." In Saint Cloud, this culture of sharing meals is gradually diminishing because of people being very busy in the hectic American lifestyle.

Why No Menus

When I go to an American restaurant, a waiter asks me what I would like to drink. While the waiter is getting the drink, I can browse through a glossy menu. However, this does not happen at the six Somali-owned restaurants in Saint Cloud. Most do not have a printed menu; some have a board on the wall that describes the food and shows their prices. Many of my close American friends who are unfamiliar with Somali food have told me that ordering at Somali restaurants is difficult. They say they do not know much about the food, and most restaurants do not have menus to educate them. On top of that, most waiters have zero or limited English skills. I can see the total confusion on their faces when they order food. Every time I ask Somali restaurant owners about this complaint from non-Somalis, they tell me they mainly cater to Somalis, so they do not have to print menus. Many Somali restaurant owners simply do not understand the importance of a menu. In my opinion, even if their customers are primarily Somalis, they should have a menu that describes the variety of foods and their prices.

When a customer enters any Somali restaurant in Saint Cloud, the waiter automatically asks if the diner wants "goat and rice," "chicken and rice," "beefsteak and rice," or "fish and rice"; pasta is another choice. In most Saint Cloud Somali restaurants, the meal also comes with a salad, banana, and bottled water or freshly mixed fruit juice. Non-Somali customers may be surprised when they are not given any option to order drinks. Most Somali waiters will hand the customer a bottle of water or a glass of juice to drink while waiting for the order to come.

At Somali restaurants, breakfast is served between 7:00 and 9:00 a.m., lunch between noon and 2:00 p.m., and dinner sometime between 6:00 and 10:00 p.m. Some restaurants like Mogadishu and Somali Café and Restaurant open at 8:00 a.m.

My white friends tell me they feel awkward seeing so many men lounging around in the Somali restaurants. Sometimes many rowdy men cluster on sidewalks close to Somali mini-malls. Some don't move out of the way for other shoppers walking by. Somali women visitors also feel uncomfortable going to traditional Somali restaurants for food and have a problem with the men who often loiter around to watch news or European soccer tournaments from Somali television channels. After they get off work, Somali men flock to restaurants in the neighborhood because these are social gathering places.

Somalis Love Tea

Any time you visit a Somali family, tea is always available in a teapot. Somali people from various regions may favor different varieties of flavorings and spices; traditionally, Somalis add spices like cloves, cardamom, cinnamon, and fresh ginger to their tea. Some add milk (*Shaah Adeis*) while a few may choose to have black tea only (*Shaah Bigeis.*)

Somali men drink afternoon tea, better known in Somali as *Asariya*. Friends talk over tea with sweet pastries, cakes, samosas, and fritters. Some women also congregate at their homes to have an afternoon tea. They chat and exchange news.

Generosity and Hospitality

Offering guests hospitality is a very important component of Somalis' everyday lives. One old Somali proverb comes to my mind whenever people talk about how generous Somalis are: "*Deeqsinimo ammaan baa laga helaa,*" which literally means, *Generosity begets praising.*

When I came to America, I used to go out for a coffee or dinner with my friends and colleagues. I was very startled those first months to see some of my friends paying their own bill. Back home, we don't have a culture of "splitting the check." In fact, it is common to see Somali friends competing with one another over paying for the meal. Somalis are extremely hospitable and generous. If one person recommends asking for separate checks, his friends may accuse him of breaking the traditional Somali generosity etiquette and becoming "Americanized."

Somali people offer hospitality to their guests, believing that they should be made welcome irrespective of their clan affiliation, skin color, and religion. The host provides guests with whatever food and drink are available because providing hospitality toward guests is one of the noblest characteristics a person can display. When a guest comes to a person's home, he or she is offered a chair, food and drink, and anything else he or she requires. If several people eat together, it is appropriate to honor the guest by serving him or her first.

Even today, when a new family arrives in Saint Cloud from a refugee camp, the community donates dry goods, curtains, carpets, and utensils. For the newcomers to get settled and acclimated to their new neighborhood, the neighbors help them with school registration, job seeking, and other necessities. Ali Osman, a recent refugee from a camp in Ethiopia, told me his new neighbors give his family rides to and from the grocery store, hospital, and school.

In the rural area in which I was born and raised, communities extended their hospitality to traveling pastorals. If the man is moving with his herds to a good pastureland and then the night falls, the host will offer him free food and accommodation and take care of his animals. On entering the house, the traveler is given a praying mat and a calabash full of water that is used for administering ablution. It is the duty of the host family to make their guests feel at home and comfortable. By the morning, the host provides the traveler with beef jerky fried with ghee and a gourd brimmed with water.[1]

Initially, Mr. Ali thought Somalis in America had abandoned their culture of hospitality and generosity. He now realizes most Somalis in Saint Cloud have preserved their ancestral cultural values as much as those in Africa have. He concluded his remark with an old Somali saying, "*Samataliye Sedkii Waa Janno,*" which literally means, *Those who do good end up in a paradise.*

Somali people usually stay in relatives' homes and apartments when they must go out of town. Even those professionals who go on conference or business trips far from home stay with their relatives until their trip ends. The reason has nothing to do with saving money. It is the Somali people's culture. Abdi Mahad, who travels much, said:

Many times, I stay in the conference hotel and hide myself from my relatives. I just do not like bothering people. I know the fact that Somali people enjoy having a planned or unplanned guest. Some family members and relatives call me when they see a social media post that my connecting flight is canceled. "Hey, come and stay with us for a few hours." You are always welcome to a Somali house.[2]

I've also noticed and experienced hospitality among the Somali community here in Saint Cloud. Every time I go out for a walk, Somalis pull over in their cars and offer me a ride. The culture of driving each other around is not alien to the Somali culture. In Africa, people often help each other with transportation. Because of Somalis' deep kindness, some may give rides to strangers. I myself have given free rides to Somali or non-Somali strangers many times. However, a few Somalis may note that it is not safe to do this. Unfortunately, not all people are trustworthy.

Greeting

Somali Americans have many types of greetings. Some are religious or culture based. Most Somalis commonly use a Muslim greeting, "*As-salamu Alaikum,*" which means, *Peace and blessing be upon you,* and return the greeting with, "*Wa alaikum assalam,*" meaning, *Peace be upon you too.* This type of greeting is for Muslims only.

Per the teachings of Islam, shaking hands with members of the opposite sex is not permissible. Because of such strict law, many conservative Muslims do not shake hands with members of the opposite gender. Some women allow handshakes. If you are being introduced to a Somali woman, wait to see if she extends her hand. If not, do not initiate a handshake. When a woman refuses to extend her hand to a man, it is not her intention to be rude; she is following her religious beliefs. Some devout Somali men avoid shaking hands with women. Some men bow their head a little bit and place their right hands on their hearts.

Sometimes, handshakes can last a long time. Some Somali men may forget that they are still holding one's hand. Always shake hands with your right hand. The left hand is considered impure. Two close male or female friends holding hands is commonplace in the Somali culture and does not raise eyebrows as much as in American culture. Somali culture always centers on openness, sociability, and communality.

Somalis often want to know how you and your family are doing. One of my white colleagues asked me why Somalis ask him about his family's health all the time.

He said he feels uncomfortable talking about this. "The tendency to talk much comes from Somali people's rich nomadic oral tradition," said Abdi Mahad. "Asking so many questions may make non-Somalis uncomfortable to continue discussing their families with someone whom they have recently met."

In Somali culture, we do not say "Hi" only. I used to say "Hi" to my fellow Somalis until they confronted me and informed me that this greeting implied I was not the least bit interested in their personal lives. Many Somalis told me they did not find Somalis' profuse greetings bizarre and intrusive. I then realized Somalis who still cling to their formal way of greeting may find the American manner of greeting peculiar as well. I see that many Americans think it's intruding into their personal space to be asked so many questions about their families. However, Somalis are communal and sociable, and our culture is caring and compassionate. Therefore, Somalis are interested in their friends' well-being.

Hand Gestures

One day I was talking to a close friend, and she told me I used numerous hand gestures while speaking. I asked her if my gestures matched my message well or distracted the audience. She said they emphasized my speech. From that day, I started observing Somalis' hand gestures and their meanings. I learned that some hand gestures used by Somalis and central Minnesotan-born natives may not mean the same thing, but many do.

For example, a thumbs-up in Somali culture may mean things are okay or signal that what you're saying is good. A thumbs-down means the opposite. When parents wiggle an index finger at their child up and down repeatedly, that may be a warning. When people wiggle their index fingers side to side, that may mean refusal. Some Somali people may not express gratitude verbally, but they place the palms of their right hands on their chests, close their eyes, and bow their heads—which means, *Thank you.* When a Somali person repeatedly snaps fingers, he or she is referring to something that happened a long time ago. For some Somalis, snapping fingers may mean, *Let's hurry up.* It is disrespectful to curl the index finger to call someone toward you. In Somali culture, such a gesture is considered offensive and belittling. It is rude to look at your wristwatch repeatedly while talking to a Somali. He or she may assume you are signaling them to leave you; for many, such a gesture may indicate the end of the conversation. In Somali culture, conversations go on for hours. Shaking one's head from side to side may mean, *No.* Shaking one's head up and down slowly may mean, *I agree with all you're saying.* Clutching the chin with the thumb and the index finger may mean, *I am thinking.* When someone's hand is on his cheek and his brows are creased, he may be in deep stress. Stroking the chin may mean someone is thinking about something. Pulling an earlobe can mean, *I have not heard anything you said.* So, in multiple ways, nonverbal communication through gestures is very similar between Somalis and the native white community.

Communication

Somalis value oral communication more than written communication. When people are holding an event, they call their guests instead of sending them a group e-mail. Some Somali people have told me that they prefer talking because they believe such a form of communication can convey opinions easier and faster and bring instant feedback.

Eye Contact

The beliefs and practices of Somalis and Americans differ regarding eye contact. Many Americans like to use direct eye contact to indicate that they are listening. Somalis, either men or women, do not directly look others in the eye. Some women may interpret a man's stern gaze as flirtation.

The culture of looking down symbolizes respect among many cultures in Somalia. For example, when a parent is scolding a child, the child is supposed to look down because of respect for his or her parents. When a child looks up into the eyes of his or her parents, Somalis may assume the child is challenging their authority and displaying disrespect and disobedience.

Somalis who have been living in America for a while may not have trouble looking a person in the eye. Even those who were born and raised in big cities and towns in Somalia may look you in the eye.

Aversion to Drawing

Saint Cloud art teachers may have seen that there are restrictions for Somali students in class. Many traditional families refuse to let their children draw, paint, or sculpt the human form. In Somali culture, we are not supposed to portray any living animal or human being. Instead, we prefer sketching things like flowers and trees. When I asked why it is not permissible for children to learn how to draw, some Somali Muslim religious leaders (*sheikhs*) informed me that the Prophet Mohammed orders Muslims not to draw humans and animals. If they do, God will ask them to bring them to life in the hereafter.

Aversion to Celebrating Birthdays

Most Somalis born and raised in rural areas do not celebrate birthdays. Some might not even know their birthdays because they do not follow the Gregorian calendar. In some rural areas, a Somali or Islamic lunar calendar is used. In Somalia, some celebrate birthdays and some do not. Abdi Mahad explained why Somalis do not celebrate birthdays or record children's dates of birth:

> Some Muslims claim that birthday celebrations have pagan roots, so should not be observed for that reason. Because of their individual preference, many Somalis from rural or urban areas choose not to celebrate their birthdays. I personally do not celebrate my birthday. It's not because of religion, culture, education, or socioeconomic status. I don't like counting my age each year. Many others start celebrating their kids' birthdays once they have arrived in the US. Despite the fact that older parents and grandparents are diametrically opposed to such celebration, the young people who are either born or raised in the US tend to throw a huge birthday party.[3]

Superstitious Beliefs

Even though most Somalis are devout Muslims who oppose superstitions, some do, to an extent, have bizarre superstitious beliefs. I still hear some in the Somali culture here. "In Somalia, taboos have interwoven into people's psyches. Regardless of Somali people's exposure to the Western world, the belief in taboo is sometimes difficult to disregard once imbued within our culture from early infancy. Belief in superstition greatly depends on regions of origins, generation, educational background, and whether or not people are from rural or urban backgrounds," said Abdi Mahad.

I collected many superstitions, but I am sharing those you may encounter. Sometimes when you speak to a Somali in the bathroom, he or she may not reply to you. This is not to be mean or rude. Bathroom talk is forbidden because it is believed to bring bad luck.

If you bite your tongue when eating, people may assume that someone else is talking about you.

Some animals bring bad luck—a black cat crossing your path, for example. When an owl lands on the top of your house, it is bad luck signifying death or a loss of financial security.

It is bad luck to start sewing a garment, or fixing a button on it, when you are wearing it. Some communities claim sewing such a shirt or dress brings destitution.

Another superstition is that one cannot sew a garment at night. Such sewing leads to bad luck. In some locations, tailors close their shops before the sunset to avoid this.

Throwing trash out at night is a nightmare for many Somalis. I avoid doing so. Somalis believe trash cans are the houses of ghosts; we avoid them at night. To prevent bad omens, some Somalis throw trash out at night while reading prayers: "I seek refuge in Allah from spirits."

Somalis believe it is unwise to put your hands over your head. Many think it portends death.

Many Somali people avoid talking about future success. It is considered bad luck when one starts boasting about his or her achievement or incoming job. That is why Somalis choose to be silent until the success has been achieved. They believe talking about your achievements will lead you to get the evil eye.

Many Somali parents, particularly mothers, avoid feeding their babies entrails, fearing that they will not learn to speak well. New mothers are advised against giving their babies an animal tongue as food, because it delays speaking. During pregnancy, some mothers crave a certain food and believe if such food is not given to her, her child will have too many birthmarks, freckles, and moles.

To treat a baby's hiccups, Somalis think you should wet a small piece of thread and plaster it on the baby's forehead. Mothers strongly believe that the thread on the child's forehead prevents further hiccupping.

Some superstitious beliefs bring good omens. If your right palm itches, you are going to get some money.

Hair Dyeing

My close friend asked me why some old Somali men dye their beards orange and how long the hair color could last. She wanted to know if bright orange or red color in men's hair had any cultural or religious significance or was a personal choice. A couple of my uncles told me they wanted to follow Prophet Mohammed's tradition of dyeing his hair and beard with henna. They told me that Muslim men aren't allowed to dye their hair with any color other than henna. I hear often that the use of henna is harmless because it contains no chemical additives detrimental to human skin.

Older Somali women dye their hair with henna to make themselves look younger. Both young and old women also apply henna on their hands, feet, and fingernails. Most henna designers say that henna lasts two to four weeks on the skin, depending on the quality and type of henna paste applied.

Naming

One of my close white friends told me she met a Somali man who was called Mohammed Mohammed. Like many Americans, she was confused by Somali names. In turn, the naming practices of white Americans also confuses Somalis.

Somali children traditionally take their father's first name and their grandfather's first name. For example, a boy's name is Ali, his dad's name is Omar, and his grand-dad's name is Ibrahim. Therefore, the full name of the child is Ali Omar Ibrahim. Apart from taking the father's name, children take their father's clan identity. In Somalia, clan affiliation is primarily along male lines.

When praying for a deceased person during eulogy, people mention the person's name along with his or her mother's maiden name. For example, Abdi ibn Fatima, which means, *Abdi, the son of Fatima.* "This practice is not limited to Somali Muslims; Jewish people also do so," said Abdi Mahad.

Somalis do not use first name and second name. For any Somali who carries a first name that is similar to his last name, like Mohammed Mohammed, the name of his father is omitted. Two siblings should not share the same name. Somalis have distinctly male or female names, while some Somalis have names that can be used by a person of either sex.

Calling a Somali person by his or her last name may cause confusion. For example, one day I was waiting in the hospital lounge and a nurse called out, "Mohamed" more than twice. I immediately looked around. All I saw was one Somali woman in her thirties and many other non-Somalis. I asked the Somali woman's name and her last name. She told me her last name was Mohamed. The woman wanted to be called by her first name, not her last name. Both the patient and the nurse were confused about the naming system. When calling your Somali students or patients, use their first names.

It is common for one person to have many names. During the naming ritual, family members who disagree with the name assign the baby other names. For example, my name is Hudda, which means, *right guidance*, but some of my family members call me Filsan, which means, *a woman with beauty*. My traditional name is Hawa, *Eve*, the first woman. I was also the firstborn child of my family. However, I choose Hudda because that name seems to fit my idea of who I am.

Somali women do not change their names at marriage. They continue to retain their father's and grandfather's names. The few Somali women who marry non-Somalis typically take their husband's family patronym upon marriage. This is very uncommon. The Somali community scorns any woman found taking her husband's name. The larger community is averse to altering their names because the traditional naming system mirrors Somalis' religion, nationality, and ethnicity. A few Somali Americans have anglicized their names. Some young men and women choose American-sounding names that differ from those chosen by their parents, like "Moha" for "Mohammed."

Somali names reflect the people's roots in the Islamic religion and Somali culture. Therefore, most names bear spiritual significance to people. For example, a first baby boy is named Mohammed, while the name Fatima, the first daughter of the Prophet Mohammed, is often given to a firstborn daughter. Apart from Mohammed, almost all males take other religious names, such as Ahmed—*one who constantly thanks God*—or Abdi, which means *servant*. The most common male names in Somalia are *Mohammed*, *Abdi*, *Abdullahi*, *Hassan*, and *Hussein*, and the most common female names are *Fatima*, *Mariam*, *Khadija*, and *Asha*.

In Somali culture, when a child is named after a messenger, prophet, local saint, or an ancestor with good morality and character, it is hoped the child will take after that person when he or she grows up.

Somali parents also name their kids after the prophets and messengers in the Bible, like Ibrahim (Abraham),

Musa (Moses), Ciise (Jesus), Daud (David), Zakariya (Zechariah), Harun (Aaron), Ilyas (Elias/Elijah), Isaaq (Isaac), Yahya (John), Yunis (Jonah), and Yusuf (Joseph).

Marriage, Conception, and Pregnancy

Many times, I am asked why Somalis marry early and have many children while young. I explain that not all Somali men and women marry early. Some choose not to enter marriage at all. I will start with the definition of marriage in Somali culture.

In Somali tradition, marriage is generally considered a union of one man and one woman to establish a home. Children born to the married couple are recognized as legitimate offspring. Most Somalis perceive marriage as a strong alliance between two different families and kinship groups. The Somali word for marriage, *guur*, is derived from the root word, *guurid*, which means, *a change of location*. This means the recently married woman moves away from her parents' home to her new matrimonial home.

Even though Islamic law is an integral part of marriage, within the Somali community, old Somali customs and traditions have a big influence on dating, bride wealth, elopement, engagements, weddings, and marriage.

Legal Age of Marriage

The legal age for marriage in Somalia is eighteen years for both men and women. However, some Somalis do not follow this law. The practice of marrying girls at a young age is most common in Somali rural areas and is sometimes found in metropolitan areas. Once a girl has reached puberty, she is considered ready for marriage. Parents encourage their children not to put off marriage, because they believe an early marriage will prevent sexual promiscuity. Many Somalis value virginity before marriage. It is still common among parents to do all they can to protect their daughters from casual sexual relations. Most of the pressure for marriage is due to cultural norms and financial constraint rather than religion. The prevalence of patriarchy in Somalia encourages older men to seek younger wives. Girls in poor families are under considerable pressure to start a relationship during their teenage years. "Sometimes a girl can get married at fourteen, fifteen, or sixteen with parental consent," said Abdi Mahad. "Poor girls and women in rural areas and those who do not have an education tend to marry younger than those in urban areas. Primarily, two factors accelerate early marriages: poor education and financial limitation on the part of the girl's family."

Early marriage is less common among Somalis in the United States. Marriages take place later in life. Somali Americans prioritize getting a good education first.

What Does *Dowry* Mean?

In Somalia, people consider a *dowry* (a gift of money or property) an obligatory Islamic and cultural practice. It is the man's responsibility to pay a dowry and other expenses incurred during the wedding ceremony. Such a payment is a part of the marriage contract and shows the girl's family that the man is serious about marrying their daughter.

There are no specific rules that state a minimum or maximum amount of dowry. Abdi Mahad explained:

In some Somali cultures, a woman's age, virginity, locality, or clan may govern payment of high dowry. Dowry can be paid in cash or in kind by the bridegroom's family to the bride's family. In Somali rural areas, the husband-to-be offers the girl's family fifty to one hundred camels. In the West, men pay between $6,000 and $50,000, depending on the man's wealth. Women have the right to decide the amount of money to be given by the husband.

In Islam, women are encouraged not to demand a huge dowry beyond the husband's means.[4]

Polygamy

I was attending a conference when a stranger sat beside me. He asked me whether polygamy was common among Somali men. I explained that there are some families who practice polygamy, but the number of couples in such a marriage is few. Polygamy is accepted among some non-Somali societies, but the practice of marrying more than one or two wives is not that common among the Somali people.

The conditions that Islam attaches to marrying multiple wives are very strict. The Islamic faith does not encourage polygamy. The Quran encourages men not to marry more than one wife unless they know they are capable of loving and treating all of them equally. This means the man must be able to provide for them financially, emotionally, and physically. The Quran also prohibits polygamous husbands from showing a preference for a particular wife. Abdi Mahad explained:

The man in a polygamous relationship is religiously expected to spend the same amount of time with each of his wives, buy them the same clothes, and treat them and their kids correspondingly. I don't think it is easy for any Muslim man to do so. If men are afraid of failing to be fair to their wives, then they must give up their notion of marrying many wives at the same time. Polygamy is not one of the five pillars that each practicing Muslim is supposed to abide by to the letter. God will not punish men if they marry one wife, but God will punish a man if he marries multiple wives and he fails to treat them all equally.[5]

A man who intends to marry another wife should consult his first wife and seek her consent. Because of the stringent rules and guidelines of polygamy, it is very rare to see polygamous relationships.

Arranged Marriage

In some societies, parents or extended family members arrange marriages. Sometimes parents do not consult their children about their marriage. In Somali culture, a successful marriage is of the greatest importance. Traditionally, Somali parents arrange their child's marriage to someone from the same clan and lineage who they know can provide a good home for their child and grandchildren. Because of family pressure, young men and women rarely marry outside of their clan. When young couples get married, they live in and near their parents' homes. If young couples fight, their parents or grandparents will intervene and work out any disagreements they may have.

Abdi Mahad said this about arranged marriages in Somali culture:

> Many Somalis continue to practice arranged marriages based on coercion. The irony here is that Islam forbids Muslims to force a girl to get married against her will. If someone does that, then it is against Islamic laws. In some Somali communities, the parents of the couple may bring up the initial idea of an arranged marriage, but they seek consent to such marriage from both young partners. If their children refuse the marriage offer, then the parents will keep looking for someone else suitable for marriage. However, suitability for marriage does not only depend on one's appearance or wealth but also on a person's social standing, personality, class, affinity, and many other traits. The parents' involvement indicates that they view marriage as a family matter, not a couple's matter. In many clans, marriage between some first cousins is preferred. This

reminds me of an old Somali proverb that says, *"Waxaad taqaano guurso, waxaa taqaano aa dhashiyee,"* which means, *Go marry someone whose background you know so that you will produce progenies whose roots you know.* In order to prevent women and men marrying someone unfamiliar, parents usually feel more secure having their children marry kin close to them. Almost all Somali clan members prefer to marry someone within their close lineages.[6]

First- and second-cousin marriage is acceptable among some Somalis, as it is among some non-Somalis. However, I do not think many Somalis are still practicing this type of marriage in the West today. Many Somalis believe cousin marriage may put the health of their offspring at risk and accelerate genetic diseases. Because of these and other negative perceptions of marriage between close relatives, young Somali men and women are avoiding marrying someone so close to them.

Many factors contribute to the decline of early and arranged marriages in the United States: women gaining economic independence, the weakening of parents' influence in their children's lives, the pursuit of college education, and the shrinking of good-paying job opportunities. While interviewing people for my book, I learned that the average

age at marriage for both Somali men and women in the United States is rising. Now it is very rare for boys and girls to marry early here. I also met Somali women who stay unmarried longer. As communities get good educations, the institution of arranged marriage among cousins decreases very rapidly. Many young Somali men and women reject their parents making their marital choice. Those Somalis who were born and raised in America now consider their first or second cousins as biological brothers and sisters. This means they avoid cousin marriage like a plague. Somali men also focus on studying and working harder to attain their American Dream of good education and financial independence. Because of these conditions, Somali families are undergoing major changes as the majority of young Somali men and women have the free will to date and marry whomever they want without their parents' involvement.

Pregnancy

In Somali society, pregnancy within marriage is greeted with joy. Most devout Somali couples do not practice child spacing or use contraceptive methods, because multiple births are encouraged. A mother of nine once said to me, "The sanctity of human life is based on procreation." So, the mother's status is elevated by the number of children she has. Another woman said, "As a mother, I consider having many children as a perfect gift from God."

Many Somali families I interviewed said that only God could determine the size of their families. One married Somali woman said, "I've met way too many young Somali couples who rely on the use of conception-control devices or procedures to space or delay children. But my husband and I are devout Muslims who decry such procedures as sinful. We will have one child or ten children exactly at the time God wants us to have them whether we use contraceptives or not."

Most Somalis observe rites associated with the new pregnancy; some are religious rites performed to bless the mother-to-be and the unborn baby. In some southern regions, the mother-to-be is given a protective amulet with Quranic inscriptions to wear through the full term of her pregnancy. The wearer believes charms may ward off evil eyes, miscarriage, and premature births.

Most Somali expectant mothers prefer not to know the gender of the baby prior to birth. Some mothers said it would not be permissible in Islam to find out the gender of their unborn children. I also know of non-Somali mothers who choose not to learn whether their first child is a boy or girl.

Traditionally, when a new baby is born, the family of the child in Africa observes a naming custom known as a *Wanqal* (pronounced as "one-cull"), the slaughtering of a male sheep for a feast to seek a blessing for the new-born baby. This custom signifies the complete acceptance of the newborn into the family membership. Therefore, its observance is mandatory for parents, particularly the child's father. The ritual is held on the sixth or seventh day to mark the arrival of the child. At the ceremony, the child is officially given his or her name in front of the invited guests and relatives. Somalis in central Minnesota and the Saint Cloud area do not observe this custom. Some may consider it an old tradition.

Abdi Mahad described some practices related to the naming of the newborn children:

> For centuries, Somalis have had a unique cultural practice known as *Gordaadin*, which means the newborn baby is taken out for the first time; the ceremony is commonly conducted on the fortieth day after the birth of the child. This day is the first time the mother and the baby leave the house to come out in public. The baby boy is given to a man chosen for his personal qualities and characteristics, such as education, honesty, diligence, bravery, decency, eloquence, and parental obedience, and the baby girl to a woman who has the same attributes.

Then the person delegated with this ritual takes the child out with a valuable object, such as a copy of the Quran or a textbook. In some rural areas, the objects selected could be used for farming, pruning, weeding, or harvesting. During this ritual, the person carries out the baby while chanting, "*Saan yeelo yeel Santayda raac,*" which means, *Do as I do and follow my footsteps.* The parents believe that their child will possess the same character, personality, and education of the person who carries out their baby for the first time. For wealthy families, the ceremony concludes with a feast to welcome the baby into the world. This "child-carrying" ritual is waning among the Somali community in the West today. Even though most Somalis name their babies on the seventh day after the birth, some families have the custom of waiting until the carrying ritual on the fortieth day after the birth of the child.[7]

Family Structure

In patriarchal and traditional structure, the man is the head of household and the breadwinner as well. The man is expected to take care of his family financially. If the father is absent or deceased, the eldest male in the family resumes the authority of the family. The oldest child carries a huge burden to take care of his younger siblings.

In most rural areas, women stay at home and raise children. In big cities, men and women work outside of their home.

Traditionally, the Somali family does not only comprise parents and children but also grandparents, aunts, uncles, and cousins. The Somali family structure is always extended. In Somalia, three generations typically live together, with the grandpa in charge of maintaining family traditions and moral values. It is still common to see extended Somali family members living together today in Saint Cloud, though it is not as prevalent as in the past. Today in central Minnesota, we see more nuclear families consisting of two parents and children; single-parent families are increasing among Somalis as well. Often a single parent family is a mother with her children.

Many Somalis believe children in nuclear families are more likely to abandon their culture and traditional way of life than are children in extended families. Most teenagers continue to live with their parents until they get married.

Respect for the Elderly

In the words of William Conton, "Africans generally have deep and ingrained respect for old age, and even when we can find nothing to admire in an old man, we will not easily forget that his gray hairs have earned him the right to courtesy and politeness."[8] Somalis are no exception. For Somalis, age is considered as an asset, which is why elders are respected. Parents often teach their children to show respect to seniors because they are the carriers of tradition, knowledge, and wisdom. Elders are often referred to as "aunt" or "uncle" even if they are strangers.

Even though Somali elders do not carry the same level of respect in the United States as they do in Somalia, many young Somalis here still have deep-rooted appreciation for seniors. But not all—one interviewee, Saeed, said:

Back home, anyone in the neighborhood could discipline our children. This reminds me of a traditional African proverb, which says, "It takes a village to raise a child." When Somalis moved to the US, kinship terminology changed. Most children who were born or brought here young avoid calling old people "aunts" and "uncles." Our children today show lack of respect for older people.[9]

When community members fight, the families go to their respective elders. The elders from different clans and subclans can meet, share experiences, and mediate the problems.

The elders also resolve conflict between family members and couples and address issues in the community and schools.

Clan and Clannism

One afternoon, I was coming out of my office when two women approached me. One of the women said that we all shared a clan membership. I looked them in the eye and told them my parents raised me to respect all kinds of people regardless of their clan, race, gender, age, and religion. From that day forward, I began to examine the effects of clannism among Somalis in Saint Cloud.

Even though all Somalis belong to the same tribe, either *Sab* or *Samaale*, we belong to different clans and sub-clans. Each sub-clan shares a common ancestor. In Somali society, clans serve as a source of solidarity and trust. During conflicts between clans, clan members protect one another, fight for better access to water and pasture, and help with ascension to political power. Members of the same clan aid one another if drought or other natural disasters occur. When one member loses all his cattle, the other members in the clan collect donations. In peacetime, clan members intermarry.

For Somalis, clan membership is the most significant social and economic structure. The clan is like life insurance, and it influences where Somalis want to live.

When new arrivals come to America, they choose to move into areas where their clan is heavily concentrated. Somalis who are already established in America help newcomers from their clan start their lives near their families, often providing a place to live until the newly arrived can stand on their own. Once the newcomers find work, they assist others who come after them. When a clan family line lives in the same neighborhood, its members assist one another. If one of them loses his job, his fellow clan members give him a place to live and food to eat until he finds a new one. This unity helps them preserve the ancestral culture and traditions that are so important to them. This cohesive community structure has helped hundreds of Somali Americans in Saint Cloud adapt and succeed.

This type of clan unity is positive because people are assisting one another. Nevertheless, clan allegiance becomes divisive and detrimental when its members politicize and polarize clans.

Among the Somali community, younger generations do not like clan linkage as much as old and middle-aged adults do. I spoke to many young men and women who said they were not raised in households that talked about clan allegiance. Some others admitted they had avoided dealing with the clan issues that still surround them. Only a few said their families taught them to treat everyone the same, no matter their clan background. Fatima Dau'ud, who was born in the United States, said, "I didn't know anything about my neighbor's clan. We just went to school together, played together, and called people by their names. When we get older, clan connection will become less of an issue. Members of our young generation will be more educated and rely on their education and career more than their clan network."

Abdi Mahad explained about Somali people's collective obligation to mutually assist through kinship groups:

Somali people came to the US with the effects of conflict and subsequent trauma that were born out of displacement and long exposure to refugee life in the neighboring countries of Kenya and Ethiopia. Before they recovered from their negative experiences, they were exposed to poor housing, poor-paying jobs, and many other problems in their new home. Many said that they had a hard time adjusting to the American way of life because of language and cultural barriers. To overcome their obstacles, the distressed Somalis resorted to counting on kinship group assistance. Somalis' kinship identity commands people to favor their patrilineal clan members more than others. Customarily,

Somali men and women take their father's name and clan identity, and they are more allegiant to their father's clan than their mother's. Men and women who are found distancing their clan members face ostracism in the community. If a member of the clan requires your moral and financial support, you are required to be there for him or her no matter what. Some clans in the United States collect some money, and such money goes to their members in case they have problems, such as illness and death.[10]

When asked how clans operate in the United States, Abdi Mahad explained further:

I will give a simple model of the typical Somali clan: we have clan A, clan B, and clan C in Saint Cloud. Each patrilineal clan whose members are descended from a common mythological ancestor has subgroups. Clan A has subgroup A1, subgroup A2, and subgroup A3. Members of subgroup A1 will have their own mutual assistance. If a member from subgroup A1 is attacked by someone from clan B, all members within clan A will unite and form a force to safeguard their members. Sometimes members of clans A, B, and C may form a symbiotic relationship that is based on the need for collaboration to solve a big problem one clan alone cannot solve.[11]

What Somalis Like about Their Culture

I asked a group of Somali men and women what they liked best about their culture; here are their answers:

Anab, a twenty-seven-year-old woman:

> Somalis are family oriented, friendly, entrepreneurs, and business savvy. Somali older people love poetry while young ones watch sports. We are proud of our faith and culture. Somalis are very kind people. People collect money to help those who are not working. Some working Somali-born mothers who are unable to pay day care fees leave their kids in the care of their parents, relatives, friends, or sometimes neighbors free of charge. Now I am a mother with two daughters. I see many Somali wives in my neighborhood who stay home to care for kids rather than work outside the home. However,

my husband and I work because I feel like we need to pay the bills. My husband's mother lives with us, so she stays home to care for my kids.

Ali, a thirty-one-year-old man:

Somalis are generous, hospitable, have a great sense of humor, and hold on to their culture to the hilt. Most Somalis do not show up on time. We ask our non-Somali friends too many questions that I think they can't answer. We don't say hi to people; we want to get to know how they are doing, how their family is doing, and everything about them. We don't consider this bad. We think it is good because we care about our friends and their family members alike.

Zeinab, a twenty-year-old woman:

Somalis are blunt. They tell you what is on their mind. If you ask them how this dress makes me look, they tell you the exact way you look, no sugarcoating. Some other cultures may assume they are rude and mean. We value our families and relatives. The Somali family is valued for its generosity. If a neighbor comes to your home and you don't give him or her a cup of tea or food, then the neighbors will ostracize you just because of your unwelcoming habit. In rural areas, your daughters and sons will remain unmarriageable. An old Somali proverb says, *"Weji furan ayaa la galaa ee albaab furan lama galo,"* which literally means, *Do not go into an open door [of your neighbor], go into a house where the host has a friendly and welcoming face.* Somalis travel back to their homeland to stay connected with their relatives. In the United States, Somalis stay near Somalis for their entire lifetimes so they can help one another.

Death and Dying

The death and dying of a family member or loved one is an emotional process. Most Somali families have burials within twenty-four hours after the death. Muslims consider the world a temporary place; when the soul departs the body, there is no need to keep the body in the world. Because of such conviction that the world is nothing but a transitory abode, people bury their dead immediately. In some cases, families may postpone a memorial service to a time when all their loved ones can attend. This postponement happens under one condition: when the deceased has made a will specifying that he or she should not be buried until certain family members arrive from other states or countries.

Somali families may refuse to have a postmortem examination performed unless there is an investigation into the death. Oftentimes, Somalis view autopsies as a desecration of the body.

Many Somalis in America who are diagnosed with a terminal illness have a desire to be buried in the country of their ancestry.

Most Somali families do not publicize the death of their family member in the newspaper, although I was told in the past Somali newspapers had some pages dedicated to obituaries. One of the main reasons for this is the language barrier. Most Somalis do not read the local newspaper. Instead, Somalis contact the Islamic Center of Saint Cloud (ICSC) for the funeral and burial arrangements.

Somalis do not buy life insurance because they consider it not Islamic. Many others claim that usury is involved with the purchase of insurance. Thus, the money for the burial arrangement often comes from the relatives of the deceased and the close-knit Somali community.

Those of the same gender as the deceased customarily perform the washing and preparation for burial. Once the body is cleaned according to the Islamic tradition, it is covered with a white sheet and taken to the mosque for a congregational prayer service, known as *Salat al-Janazah*. After the prayer is done, the body is typically transported to North Star Cemetery in Saint Cloud for burial. In most Islamic sects, women are not allowed to attend the burial ceremony; Sufism is the only Islamic sect that allows women to go, and some Somali Muslims in central Minnesota are Sufis.

Islam encourages Muslims to participate in the funeral Mass and procession to the cemetery. After the body is buried, one of the local imams or sheikhs reads a long prayer. Some part of the prayer is as follows: "O Allah, forgive [*name of the person*] and elevate his/her rank among those who are guided. Send him/her along the path of those who came before, and forgive him/her. O Lord of the worlds, expand his/her grave and shed light upon him/her in it."

Memorial services may occur in the home. After the burial, the immediate family receives visitors, and it is common for the family to provide food for the guests. Because of the hectic working schedules of Somalis in the area, the mourning period may be shorter than the norm. Sometimes, people do not show an intense emotion because they believe in God's fate. Somalis are fatalists who believe death is inevitable. Some show patience and perseverance because they realize they have no control over death.

Wives whose husbands die avoid wearing immodest outfits, jewelry, makeup, perfume, or henna decoration up to four months and ten nights after the death, a practice known in Islam as *Iddah*. The primary wisdom behind this practice is that the recently widowed woman should respect and honor the sanctity of the marriage bond and the time she had spent with her deceased husband. During that Iddah period, the widow cannot date, marry, or go near a man. Once her Iddah expires, she is free to live her own life, to wear anything she likes, or marry any man she desires.

In Somalia, family members, relatives, neighbors, and colleagues congregate in the deceased person's home to mourn for three to seven days. The family of the dead person also mourns the date of the passing every year. In Somalia, a death anniversary is called *Hus*. Hus attendees observe the day by praying for the soul of the departed. For such occasions, the family traditionally prepares an elaborate set of dishes, including basmati rice, goat meat, camel milk, cow peas served with fried coffee beans, and so forth. After the lunch, the invited religious men recite the Quran and other prayers.

In recent years, Hus practices have changed. Owing to family separation, economic factors, and a hectic lifestyle, Somalis in Saint Cloud and central Minnesota do not celebrate the anniversary of a loved one's passing. Instead, they throw a one-day banquet for people who pay homage to the family of the deceased. This is a clear sign that the ways in which Somali Americans mourn have changed.

Festivals and Holidays

Somalis in central Minnesota observe several holidays and celebrate cultural and religious festivals. Somalis celebrate Somali independence from Great Britain on June 26 and independence from Italy on July 1. The British ruled the north of Somalia, while the Italians reigned in the south. These two days are of great importance in the history of the Somali people.

In Saint Cloud, several activities take place at Lake George each year on these two days. Somalis, both young and old, come out dressed in traditional Somali attire, carrying the Somali flag. During the celebration, they sing the Somali national anthem and patriotic songs in chorus, and they perform traditional folk dances like *Dhaanto* (sometimes pronounced as "Danto"). The festival focuses on creating cultural awareness among the members of the Somali diaspora and teaches the younger generations, who were either born or raised in America, to be connected to national holidays in their ancestral home.

Celebration of Somalia's holidays does not mean Somalis in Saint Cloud do not embrace and honor their new country's celebrations, such as Memorial Day, Independence Day, and Presidents' Day. Many Somalis I have spoken to said it was fun to celebrate America's heritage and to be mindful of where we Somalis come from.

There are many days in the Islamic calendar with distinctive religious importance. Somalis celebrate *Eid al-Fitr* to mark the end of dawn-to-sunset fasting during the entire month of Ramadan. The Eid al-Fitr is held on the first day of *Shawwal* in the Islamic calendar (see the Islamic calendar).[12] The festivities start early in the morning and last for over two days. People wake up around 5:00 a.m., take a shower, and wear new garments. Both adults and children dress in their best clothes. Muslims attend a special prayer. In Saint Cloud, Somalis congregate at the Whitney Recreation Center every year. During the special prayer, people recite their

ISLAMIC CALENDAR MONTHS

1. Muharram
2. Safar
3. Rabi' al-awwal
4. Rabi' al-thani
5. Jumada al-awwal
6. Jumada al-thani
7. Rajab
8. Sha'ban
9. Ramadan
10. Shawwal
11. Dhu al-Qi'dah
12. Dhu al-Hijjah

declaration and proclamation of faith known as *Takbir.* After the prayer, families invite their friends and neighbors to exchange gifts and eat together.

Each year, Muslims also observe *Eid al-Adha*, the Feast of Sacrifice, which commemorates Abraham's readiness to sacrifice his son Isaac and God's substitution of a ram, preserving Isaac's life. The feast is held on the tenth day of *Dhu al-Hijjah* in the Islamic lunar calendar. The Eid al-Fitr and Eid al-Adha are the most religiously significant Muslim holidays that the Somali community in Saint Cloud observe. Somalis in Saint Cloud would love to see the two Muslim holidays declared as public and national holidays. Most Somalis take time off from work and school to celebrate with their family and friends.

Language, Art, and Music

Even though Somali is spoken in a large section of East Africa, many different accents exist among Somali speakers, and most Somali regions have distinct accents that can be easily identified.

The US-born children of Somali parents speak English more than their parents' mother tongue. Children who were brought to the United States at a younger age speak "Somalinglish," mixing English with Somali. Many young children I met can speak Somali but cannot read or write it. The erosion of the Somali language is worrisome for many Somalis in central Minnesota. The parents I interviewed commonly expressed their fear that the English language would one day overtake their mother tongue as second and third generations of Somali Americans communicate via English. Because of the fear of Somali language extinction, some parents teach Somali on weekends or encourage their children to watch streaming TV stations coming live from Somalia. The Saint Cloud Somali Community FM Radio station provides Somali programs intended to preserve the Somali language.

Said Abdi Mahad, who teaches a course on conversational Somali and introduction to Somali culture:

Every state I go to visit, I see many Somali professionals who strive so hard to revitalize their dying native language. Like culture, languages are passed on from one generation to another. Central Minnesota Community Empowerment Organization (CMCEO) conducts a conversational Somali course that encourages cross-cultural communication in central Minnesota. My students want to speak a little Somali and learn Somali culture in order to connect and communicate with the growing Somali community.[13]

People are conscious of the consequences of losing their own distinctive language. Some attach language to their identity. They argue that their language is the hallmark and embodiment of their culture. When children lose such language familiarity and fluency, they lose their ancestral roots. There is a Somali saying that goes, "A community becomes extinct when its language becomes extinct." Maintaining language means maintaining more unified communities. Abdi Mahad argues:

> Our parents and grandparents are the transmitters of language. Passion for language dissemination is very high for the Somalis in America. If one looks at the history of language maintenance among early European immigrants, we can understand that language preservation is not only important to Somalis but to Scandinavians and Germans as well. The early European immigrants and their descendants continued to speak their native languages for many years, encouraging their children not to lose fluency.
>
> Somalis, like other immigrants and refugees in the US, are proud of where they come from, and they don't want their heritage and language to be eradicated. Many Somalis quote a well-known

proverb: *"Waari maysid war hakaa haro,"* which literally means, *You won't live forever, so leave a legacy.*[14]

The following poem composed by Cilmi Faradheere demonstrates the importance of holding on to one's mother tongue:

> *Nin Afkiisa daayacay,*
> *Dulli kama fogaadoo,*
> *Dabin kama baxsanayoo,*
> *Dulmi kama gashaantoo,*
> *Duni kama dhex-muuqdee,*
> *Afka yaan la daqarreyn,*
> *Oo yaanan laga didin,*
> *Waa waxaan ku duulnoo.*

> *He who deserts his mother tongue*
> *will not avoid disgrace,*
> *will not escape from a trap,*
> *will not shield from a bellicosity, and*
> *will not be visible among other communities.*
> *Do not scar your mother tongue.*
> *Do not shy away from speaking it.*
> *It is your heritage.*

Somali Oral Tradition

For centuries, the Somali people have been known to be good oral poets. The Somalis have used poetry to convey certain themes like peace, history, custom, and comments on current events. In Somalia, poetry is used to stop clan fighting and encourage youth to hang on to their cultural heritage.

Some poets also express public and personal feelings. Traditionally, Somalis passed down their history orally through stories. Somali Americans still cling to Somali folktales. Culturally, tales are generally passed down from one generation to another; therefore, Somali children and adults are acquainted with Somali folktales and fairy tales. Somali folklore is made up of ancient traditional stories, songs, music, dancing, proverbs, popular beliefs, and customs. Somali traditional stories contain an array of mythical figures, such as Egal Shidad, Arawelo, Wiil Waal, and many others. Arawelo is believed to be an authoritarian queen in Somalia who castrated men found clinging to patriarchy. Dhagdheer is believed to be a bloodthirsty cannibal who had long ears. This story bears a resemblance to the German tale of Hansel and Gretel, where a cruel witch eats children.

Music

Somalia has rich folk music that reflects the diverse cultures of the region. Somali music has many different genres and styles, and the types of music Somali people listen to may vary, depending on age and region. For example, old Somalis listen to Somali classical songs known as *Qaaraami*, while the younger generation is attracted to music with Western music notation. For Millennials, rap and reggae have become more dominant in contemporary Somali music. According to Abdi Mahad:

> Music is an important part of the Somali culture. Somalis, both young and old, prefer Somali music over other types. The St. Cloud Somali Community Radio airs popular Somali music nonstop twenty-four hours a day. For the last twenty-five years, new Somali singers came up on the stage to make great cover songs. They fused old traditional music with a touch of hip-hop and jazz. Some of these new cover songs may sound better than the originals. Today, you may hear Somali songs that are heavily influenced by Arab music or the music from countries neighboring Somalia.

Somalis mark their country's Independence Day at Lake George with music.

Religion

Islam is the third of the three revealed religions, following Judaism and Christianity. According to the Pew Research Center, there are an estimated 1.2 billion Muslims in the world today and about 3.3 million Muslims of all ages living in the United States in 2015.[15] Muslims make up less than 1 percent of the US adult population.

Muslims use the Arabic word *Allah* for God, the Almighty Creator. Muslims memorize the Quran, the holy book of Islam, at an early age. Muslims believe that the sacred writings of Islam were divinely revealed by God to the Prophet during his life at Mecca and Medina, through the Archangel Gabriel.

In Arabic, the term *Quran* (sometimes spelled as *Qur'an* or *Koran*) may have two root meanings: *al-Qar*, meaning *to collect* and *Qara*, meaning *to recite*. One of the Islamic school instructors in Saint Cloud told me:

Muslims consider the Quran to be a sacred book full of guidance. It tells Muslims what to do, things to avoid. The Quran has 30 sections (*juz*), 114 chapters (*surah*), and 6,666 verses (*ayahs*). Children learn the Quran by heart before they reach the age of fifteen. Someone who memorizes the Quran is called *hafiz*, meaning *memorizer*. In Somali culture, the Quran memorizer is highly respected.

The process of Quran memorization generally takes part-time students three to five years. Students who are able to stay full-time in Islamic schools can complete memorization in less than two years. For instance, children in rural areas who go to Islamic school full-time learn the Quran faster than those in metropolitan areas. Young Somali students in central Minnesota today might take one class or two classes on weekends, requiring only a couple of hours of in-class study time. Because of their hectic schedules, some children will never complete memorization of the Quran. I think the weekly time commitment is a major reason that it takes some children longer to memorize the Quran.[16]

It is important to define the terms *Islam* and *Muslim* here. According to Sheikh Hassan, a Muslim scholar and imam at the Islamic Center in the Lake George neighborhood of Saint Cloud:

> The Arabic word *Islam* means *submission to the will of God*. It is derived from the infinitive *aslama*, which means, *to surrender*. The Arabic word *salaam* ("peace") has the similar root as the word *Islam*. Being a true Muslim is to accept and profess the oneness (monotheism) of God. For example, the greeting *Salaam alaikum* literally means, *Peace be upon you*. The *Muslim* is the one who submits to God. Many may confuse *Islam* with *Muslim*. Islam is the religion while a Muslim is the believer or follower of the Islamic faith.[17]

Pillars of Islam

Islam has five primary obligations, known as "pillars of faith," that Muslims must practice.

1. *Shahadah*, profession of faith, is the first pillar of Islam. Muslims bear witness to the oneness of God by reciting

the creed "There is no God but Allah, and Muhammad is His Messenger."

2. *Salah*, prayer five times a day, is a religious duty for every Muslim unless they are physically and mentally unable to perform it. Prayer is the second pillar. Therefore, Muslims perform five daily prayers facing the same direction:

   a) *Fajr*, the early-morning prayer performed before sunrise (4:00 to 6:00 a.m.).

   b) *Duhr*, midday prayer (between 12:00 and 1:00 p.m.). When Muslims pray *Jumu'ah* (a special Friday prayer), they are not required to pray Duhr afterward.

   c) *Asr*, late-afternoon prayer (3:00 to 5:00 p.m.).

   d) *Maghrib*, the sunset prayer performed immediately after the sun sets.

   e) *Isha*, the night prayer, preferable to pray before midnight.

   Muslim schools of thought agree that prayer is invalid if performed before or after its appointed time. The specific praying times alter with the changing of sunrise and sunset. Today, most people have apps on their smartphones and gadgets to remind them of the prayer time with a prayer call alarm.

Women who are menstruating or women who have recently given birth are excluded from the requirement to pray. Islam also permits a Muslim to miss a prayer while traveling, but he or she will make up the prayer later.

Since practicing Muslims pray five times a day, a common question is, how long does each prayer take? For many Muslims, each prayer generally takes a little over five to eight minutes, twenty-five to forty minutes in total for the five prayer times. It's preferred that Muslims offer their prayers in a mosque, but if circumstances force them elsewhere, then they can pray anywhere as long as it's clean. Even though a person can pray alone, the Quran advises Muslims to pray in a group because it is believed that joining fellow believers has more rewards.

Women have a place in the mosque to pray separately from men. I often get asked whether a Muslim woman can lead men in prayer. In congregational prayers, men lead women.

3. *Zakat*, paying alms, is the third pillar. Only those who have been bestowed with wealth should pay alms to the poor. According to an eminent Muslim scholar in Saint Cloud, the payment of Zakat multiplies one's wealth. In Islam, wealth hoarding is prohibited.

4. *Sawm*, fasting, is the fourth pillar of Islam. Ramadan is the ninth month of the Islamic calendar. During that month, Muslims are forbidden from eating, drinking, and engaging in conjugal sexual relationships from dawn to sunset for thirty days. Muslims who are physically or mentally ill may be excused from fasting. Pregnant, breastfeeding, menstruating women, or those who are traveling, do not have to fast. Practicing Muslims also abstain from lying, gossiping, cursing, theft, and exhibiting lustful desires. These actions are believed to invalidate one's fasting. Ramadan is mandatory for a Muslim who has reached puberty (age fifteen and up). People who skip fasting because of these above-mentioned conditions should make up the fast at a later date. The main purpose of Ramadan is to teach Muslims a total devotion to God. During the month of Ramadan, devout Muslims pray *Taraweeh*, a special nighttime prayer recited in congregation.

5. *Hajj*, the pilgrimage to Mecca to be undertaken once in a lifetime.

Every Muslim should abide by six articles of Islamic faith:

- *Belief in God*
- *Belief in Angels*
- *Belief in Holy Books* (Muslims must revere all scriptures revealed to the prophets before Mohammed, which include the Torah, the Psalms, and the Gospel)
- *Belief in the Day of Judgment and Hereafter*
- *Belief in the Prophets* (Holy Quran mentions the names of twenty-five messengers and prophets, which include Adam, Noah, Abraham, Ishmael, Isaac, Moses, Jesus, and Mohammed)
- *Belief in Destiny*

What is *Wudu*?

Wudu (or ablution) is a ritual cleansing of the face, hands, and feet three times before performing the daily prayers. Here is how the ablution is performed:

- Wash the face three times. Always make sure you don't leave any parts of the face dry.
- Wash the arms (right arm first) up to the elbows.
- Rub the head with the fingers, starting from the forehead hairline to the nape.

- Clean the ears by inserting the tip of the index fingers.

- Wash the feet up to the knees (always start with the right foot and make sure that water reaches between the toes and back of the feet).

In Islam, a prayer is a physical, verbal, and spiritual act shown with humility and submission to the Creator. For a prayer to be validated, one has to follow the sequence of ritual washing. Is it mandatory for Muslims to wash five times a day prior to praying? Islamic schools of thought disagree on this. Some imams say that once you perform ablution at home in the morning, you don't have to remove shoes or socks when washing the feet during the day, so Muslim students or workers can run their wet hands over the top of their socks and shoes. Some imams argue that every Muslim is required to wash his or her face, arms, and feet. Without this type of cleansing process, one's prayer is not accepted. One imam quoted a verse in the Quran that says, "You believers, when you stand up to pray, wash your faces, and your hands up to the elbows, and wipe your heads, and your feet up to the ankles." Whether to rub the socks and shoes with wet hands or administer ablution continues to be debated among Muslim scholars.

One of the imams in Saint Cloud said:

Some scholars say one has to wipe his socks with a wet hand while others contend that it is important for one to go through all of the steps of ritual ablutions before each of their five-times-a-day prayers. Knowing all these differences, I encourage students and staff to not wash their feet in the restroom sinks if they are afraid to slip and get hurt. Safety is important. Refusing students to administer ablution restricts Muslim students' ability to practice their religion freely as specified in the US Constitution. The issue of ablution causes so much uproar in the Saint Cloud area, as some schools refuse to install foot-washing stations for their Muslim students and staff.[18]

Somalis are one ethnic group, with one language, and are almost 100 percent Sunni Muslim. According to one of the Saint Cloud area imams, "Sunni Islam is the largest denomination of Islam. Sunni Muslims believe the Prophet Mohammed did not designate a successor, whereas Shia Muslims believe the Prophet Mohammed chose his son-in-law and cousin Ali ibn Abu Talib to succeed him."

The Islamic religion is one of the most significant and uniting factors of identity among Somalis. There is no exact date for the arrival of Islam in Somalia, but many books state, "Islam came to Somalia through peaceful means long before it reached to Medina, the first capital of Islam.

It is said that some of the companions of the Prophet, who were fleeing persecution in Mecca, visited the city of Zeila (in the north of Somalia) and shared the message of Islam with people there."[19] Some other books mention that due to "a long tradition of trading connections to the Arabian Peninsula, the Somalis were converted to Islam at an early date."[20] No matter when Islam came to East Africa, most Somali people are strict in their Islamic principles.

In Saint Cloud, there are three Islamic centers. These religious institutions play active bonding and bridging roles in the lives of Somalis.

Abdi Hassan, who came to Saint Cloud in 2000, reminisces about the time Somalis did not have a mosque in the city. "We prayed together at each other's apartment buildings until we rented two bedrooms for praying." Today, Somalis do not have to worry about mosques and Quranic schools. According to Islamic Center of Saint Cloud president Mohyadin Mohamed, "The big centers currently have 350 students enrolled in after-school and weekend classes." Classes run every Saturday and Sunday from 9:00 a.m. to 1:30 p.m.

In the afternoons and evenings, the centers offer adult classes. During the summer, the centers provide full-time classes. Those courses run for six weeks. There are also small private Islamic schools—known in Somali as *Dugsi* or in Arabic as *Madrasa*—in Saint Cloud. Those Quranic schools provide

Islamic education for children between the ages of five and eighteen. Children are placed in groups according to their ages and abilities. Students learn memorization and exegesis of the Quran, Islamic jurisprudence, Hadiths, and basic Arabic language.

Some Islamic schools require children to wear a uniform, usually a white robe for boys and a *jilbab* or *abaya*, a long, loose dress with a scarf, for girls.

Islamic schools assist the children to preserve and follow the Islamic way of life. Therefore, most parents in Saint Cloud send their kids to local Islamic centers for several reasons other than studying beliefs and practices. Most parents argue that Islamic schools prevent drug use, gang violence, and disobedience. Apart from teaching Islamic principles, the Islamic Center of Saint Cloud (ICSC) was formed in 1996 to offer the Muslim communities in Saint Cloud and its surrounding areas a place for prayer, marriage and funeral services, and family counseling. The ICSC has recently begun new outreach programs, inviting Muslims and non-Muslims in Saint Cloud to get to know one another and strengthen their unity.

What is *Sharia*?

For over a decade, I have been asked, "What is *Sharia*?" The belief in God and his Prophet Mohammed are the most important components of Islam. Muslims also are required to abide by Sharia, or Islamic law. Today we hear some rumors that Somalis are conspiring to take over America, multiplying in Saint Cloud, and their Sharia law will slowly creep into the local laws and customs. The Somali Muslim community does not want to lose their religious identity; neither do they want to impose Sharia on anyone.

But first, what is Sharia? According to Sheikh Hassan:

> *Sharia* is an Arabic word that literally means, *a path or a way to be followed*. On top of that, Sharia is the religious legal system that manages and guides the members of the Islamic faith for everyday life. Some issues the Sharia covers are family, marriage, divorce, annulment, avoidance of intoxicating beverages, and abstinence of sexual relations outside of marriage.[21]

The Sharia injunctions are derived from the Quran and the Hadith, teachings and example of the Prophet Mohammed. In Somalia, people employ customary laws known as *heer* instead of Sharia. For example, in rural areas, pastoral nomads are predisposed to constant conflicts over scarce resources, pastureland, and water. To reduce stringent criminal penalties, the clan elders limited the use of Sharia to issues related to conflict. The effectiveness of the elders' traditional mechanisms in resolving disputes can be attributed to customs and norms within the heer. However, the application of Islamic law became more widespread after the civil war in 1991.

What is *Jihad*?

The term *Jihad* is one of the most misunderstood Islamic terms of all in the United States. Most of the time, Jihad is routinely translated as *holy war*. To know more about what the literal definition of this word means, I asked Sheikh Hassan, an imam in Saint Cloud. He said:

> *Jihad* has numerous meanings. It is the spiritual struggle within oneself against sin. Jihad means to strive for attaining a good moral, spiritual, or political goal. Jihad is not restricted to using violence. Overcoming sin is a type of Jihad. When you abstain yourself from worldly temptations, such as greed, lust, pride, envy, and wrath, you are in Jihad. Even though Jihad means a holy war, such a war can be engaged in for self-defense only. The Sharia has clearly restricted this kind of Jihad to certain conditions while forbidding wrongdoing of any

sort. In such a war, Muslims cannot kill or harm noncombatants. Older people, women, children, pastors, and other religious figures, or those who are unarmed go under the fold of noncombatants.[22]

What is *Hijab*?

Hijab is an Arabic word meaning *cover* or *curtain*. It also has a wider meaning like *modesty and privacy*. The term may also mean a piece of fabric that covers a Somali woman's head and neck. I'm often asked, "Why do Somali women wear a hijab? Do Somali men force women to dress a certain way?" One day I was in a seminar and a man came up to me and asked if Muslim women wearing hijabs feel like they are oppressed. I said women are not coerced into wearing a hijab; they choose to do so.

For me, the point of wearing a hijab is to be modest. I also see it as a code of conduct. I don't wear my scarf around my head as a piece of cloth. I wear it as a part of my identity. It shows others who I am. Many Somali women tell me they are proud of who they are. The hijab is something women have been wearing since they were children.

Even though not all women wear clothing according to Islamic dress code, it is important to look into why women wear the hijab. As usual, Somali clothing is a combination of traditional, African, Western, and Islamic styles. Conservative Somali women wear full-length dresses, known as *dirac*, *guntino*, and *abaya*. All these types of dresses entirely cover the body. For example, dirac is a formal dress worn in events like weddings. Guntino is a garb worn primarily by Somali women in rural areas. It consists of several yards of light material that is tied over the shoulder and draped around the body. Wearing guntino is now limited to when women are displaying their traditional attire; it is gradually disappearing in big cities.

Women wear a hijab when out in public. Somali women wear a hijab for a variety of reasons. Some women wear the hijab as a means of fulfilling God's commandment for modesty, while others wear it as a personal choice. According to Islamic principles, a girl is supposed to dress modestly when she reaches the age of fifteen. Sometimes younger girls wear a hijab. A woman covers her hair with a scarf in the presence of adult males outside of her immediate family, but when she is at home with her family members like her father, brother, or uncle, she does not have to cover her head. A woman does not have to wear a hijab at home when her husband is around.

Even though there are various types of hijab outfits, Somali women wear clothes that do not accentuate or reveal their bodies. Some women who come from families that are more conservative cover their faces in a *niqab*, a face veil. Many Muslim women choose not to cover their hair and wear jeans or other typical Western outfits with a scarf.

In Somalia in the 1980s, women did not cover their hair and most dressed like typical American women. The practice of wearing Western dress changed as Barre's government collapsed in 1991 and a group of Muslim puritans known as Wahhabis arose in the political vacuum.[23] This group of radical fundamentalists, now known as al-Shabaab, wants Somalia to go back to the period of caliphates in early Islam.

Before the current Islamic dressing style came to Somalia, only Somali women living in coastal cities and towns descended from Arabia wore *shuka*, a body-length outer dress, usually black in color.

Chapter 4

INTEGRATION AND ASSIMILATION

When you go to a land full of blind people, make yourself blind.

—Somali proverb

CENTRAL MINNESOTA IS HOME TO A GROWING Somali population that came to the United States with strong attachments to their ancestral heritage and identity. These new first-generation Somali Americans took jobs in such places as meat-packing plants and made sure their children went to school. Like the Europeans, Southeast Asians, and Mexicans who arrived before them, Somalis regularly experience struggles and challenges hindering their integration into the broader American society. However, members of the second generation tend to catch up quickly, some outdoing the native-born population. Many members of the second generation acquire college degrees and become doctors, lawyers, or engineers; others become involved in local politics. They make quicker progress in their integration. Unlike their parents and grandparents, the US-born children of Somali ethnicity may find themselves detached from the conservative traditions of the older generation.

The United States has been referred to as a "melting pot" or a "salad bowl," where countless groups of inhabitants of diverse faiths, nationalities, and ethnic backgrounds come together, having arrived from all over the world. For instance, Saint Cloud has many different religious groups, such as Lutheran, Catholic, Episcopal, Methodist, Pentecostal, Presbyterian, and others; foreign-born newcomers brought their faith with them. Each group, past or recent, has had the freedom to follow and practice its faith and unique customs, though each has experienced some degree of prejudice and discrimination. This cultural pluralism and diversity is what makes the United States so remarkable. We must be mindful of the contributions of the immigrants and refugees who made this country what it is today.

We must also be aware that each wave of immigrants and refugees struggles with the question of how much of its ancestral cultures, values, and religious practices to retain and how much of the new society's culture to adopt. Sometimes newcomers are pressured to adopt part or all the culture; sometimes they can choose freely. Immigrants and refugees also contribute something to their new home: food, clothing, music, new ideas, and so on. Likewise, while immigrants and refugees do not have to forget who they are and where they came from, they usually do need to learn the new language and values that will help them succeed in their adaptation and integration.

Melting Pot and Salad Bowl

When Israel Zangwill coined the phrase *melting pot* in the early twentieth century, he said that "all the races of Europe" would melt together. Others have argued that America never was a melting pot but rather a *salad bowl* in which its various ethnic and religious groups have had various degrees of freedom to maintain their beliefs and cultures, though they've often met prejudice against them. Native Americans and African slaves had to fight to retain their cultures; some accepted new cultural beliefs and practices and blended them with their own, such as in the rich tradition of African American Christianity.

In the United States, integration and assimilation have been part of the national immigration debate for decades and have become buzzwords in Saint Cloud and central Minnesota. What does integration mean and look like? How much must foreign-born newcomers assimilate, and which American cultural values and norms should they adopt? Are the Somalis integrating into American mainstream society? What does it mean to be an American? Do Americans share a common culture? To answer these questions, let us look into definitions of assimilation and integration.

Assimilation and *Integration* Defined

Before I go into the definitions of *assimilation* and *integration*, I want to explain the terms *first generation* and *second generation*. In this book, *first generation* means the people who were born elsewhere and came to this country, and *second generation* refers to the children of the first generation, who were born in the United States.

Every time I speak with Somalis and non-Somalis about the precise definitions of *assimilation* and *integration*, I find many misunderstandings. Therefore, I will discuss the meanings of these two terms as I am using them.

Assimilation involves the adoption of cultural values and norms from the broader society. Minority groups, immigrants, or refugees may adopt some or all the broader societies' cultural values and norms through coercion or voluntarily. Drawing from J. F. Davidio et al., and others, we can define *full assimilation* as the abandonment of cultural values and norms by a minority group, immigrants, or refugees and the full adoption of the cultural values and norms of the larger society.[1]

Integration refers to the degree of participation in the broader society, interacting with people outside of one's own racial, ethnic, or religious community—for example, finding jobs in the broader community, participating in civic associations, going to school and shopping at stores in the broader community, participating in politics, and so on. Integration assumes *cultural pluralism*—that group members may adopt some cultural values and norms from the larger society and identify with it but that they will also keep their own cultural values, norms, and identity to some degree; they do not abandon them. For example, one can be Somali and American. If one is fully assimilated, he has abandoned his group's cultural values and norms completely, and he also is interacting with people outside of his own ethnic, racial, or religious group. The individual has given up his Somali identity and fully adopted an American identity.

Another possibility is *isolation*, where individuals or groups may not assimilate or integrate to any degree; the Amish communities in the United States are an example of this. They wish to remain isolated from the broader society, preserve their religion and culture, and live and work inside their own community with minimal interaction with the outside world. One other possibility is an *identity crisis*, in which an individual is not comfortable with his group's culture or the culture of the broader society.[2] We see examples of all four of these types of relationships among Somalis in Saint Cloud, though integration is most preferred and most common among the Somalis I interviewed.

The Somali language does not have an exact literal term equivalent to assimilation. I don't think I heard the words *assimilation* or *integration* until I came to America. Somalia is a racially and ethnically homogeneous country. The first time Somalis hear these terms is when they arrive in the United States. The closest Somali term equivalent to assimilation is *milan*, which means, *to dilute*. The term is used when one makes a liquid thinner or less strong by adding water or a foreign substance, or to lessen the strength of something. Like many other refugees and immigrants, many Somalis do not want to see their culture and faith diluted by another culture. Some Somalis prefer using the word for integration, *dhehgal*, instead of *milan* because they want to be part of American society while maintaining their Somali identity.

The interviewees described the complexities of assimilation and integration. Thus, it is important to explain the differences between the metaphors of the melting pot, a more monolithic concept of culture, and the salad bowl, which means cultural pluralism.

First, what is the cultural pluralism / salad bowl model? Cultural pluralism, as noted above, says that different groups of people preserve their respective identities while integrating into the broader society. "Pluralism is mutual respect between the various groups in a society for one another's culture, allowing minorities to express their own culture without experiencing prejudice and discrimination."[3] The immigrant and refugee groups adopt some of the mainstream culture while keeping their unique cultural heritages. In the pluralistic nation, different racial and ethnic groups can live in harmony. The United States is an example of the salad bowl. Even though US citizenship is based only on the acceptance of basic principles—the Constitution—and the law, not ethnic/cultural factors like in some European countries, the concept of pluralism in America has come under attack by some critics. They argue that pluralism leads to nothing but disunity, disloyalty, and the maintenance of distinctive cultures that clash.

A version of the assimilation model is the melting pot. "The melting pot is diverse racial and ethnic groups, or both, forming a new creation, a new cultural identity."[4] Those in favor of the assimilation of the foreign born want them to shed their individual and group attributes and blend themselves into American society instead. "To create a new American culture," said Abdi Mahad, "the melting pot theory allows people from various cultures and ethnicities to come to the US and blend into the pot. This kind of melting method leads diverse cultures to become indistinguishable from one another." In the United States today, the strong emphasis is on cultural pluralism, and Somalis prefer this "salad bowl" view. According to Abdi Mahad:

> The differences between the metaphors of the homogeneous melting pot and the pluralistic salad bowl are apparent. When we mix different vegetables together, we create a new food in the fusion pot, but in a salad bowl, the assortments of vegetables don't mix; neither do they melt. Each maintains its original form, color, and identity. The advocates of melting pot theory favor the assimilationist principle, while the salad bowl proponents encourage each community to preserve its cultural identity. An anti-immigrant, anti-refugee *nativist*, on the other hand, would not want the pollution and dilution of his or her culture by foreign cultures at all.[5]

To keep the host community's culture pure, nativists, sometimes called *nationalists*, want to keep foreigners out because, they argue, the melting pot makes their culture impure and diluted. They are also very opposed to any salad bowl, needless to say; they think everyone should be like them.

Somalis' Perceptions of Assimilation and Integration

Are Somalis ready to integrate into the host country? The answer depends on whom we talk to. Among Somalis in Saint Cloud, there are different views of integration. First-generation Somalis and their children who were born or raised in the United States do not share an identical outlook with the older generation of Somalis on what integration means. First-generation Somalis who have postsecondary education and those who have little education see the process of integration through different lenses.

The vast majority of Somalis continue to be Muslim, following the faith that was brought to them at the time of the Prophet Mohammed. Proud of their religion and culture, and based on their images and understanding of the United States, the most frequent advice grandparents give their children and grandchildren as they depart Africa for America is, "If you get to the United States safely, do not ever lose touch with your ancestral identity and exchange it for a totally American identity. Cling to your culture and language as long as you live." Such advice is shared by many. On the eve of my departure for America, a group of older relatives visited me and advised me to remain among the Somali population. Understandably, parents and grandparents fear that their children or grandchildren will "melt" into American main-stream society, abandoning their own culture, language, and ethnic ties. "When the first wave of Somalis arrived in the US," said Abdi Mahad, "they tended to form ethnic neigh-borhoods. There are many reasons they did this; one reason was the fear of losing their Somali culture and identity."[6]

For many Somali community members, the notion of assimilation has a negative connotation associated with the abolition of one's identity and ancestral culture as part of a process of fully adopting American culture. Therefore, Somalis discuss to what degree they should assimilate and maintain their own culture, faith, and ancestral ways of liv-ing. The Somalis I interviewed opposed the idea of totally adopting a new value system, changing their own way of eat-ing and dressing, and anglicizing their names. "We bring our personal values and practices from our home country," said a community elder who spoke on the condition of anonymity. "We do not have to seek to transform the native culture of America; neither do we desire to give up our principles."

Even though Somali Americans are open to some forms of integration, most are diametrically opposed to comprehensive assimilation into American culture. They argue that assimilation can be a one-sided process bent on conformity with white Christian culture. "The reason why some segments of the Somali population refuse to use the term *assimilation* in their language is that it may sound like saying that your ancestors' way of living is antique; come and join our mainstream cultural identity, which is more modern and civil than yours," said Abdi Mahad. "Many chose the term *integration* over *assimilation*. Somalis would love to maintain their ethnic identity mixed with American identity."

"We Somalis prefer to integrate instead of assimilate," said Ahmed Ali, the lead staff organizer of the Greater Minnesota Worker Center. "This means we can retain the best of our identity while celebrating the best of the new culture. I can be a law-abiding American citizen while being a Muslim and Somali person at the same time. I can fully participate and be able to contribute to the community politically and economically."[7] These views are an expression of cultural pluralism.

Some Somalis told me that they have steadfastly pledged an allegiance to both the United States and their old country. According to Abdi Mahad, "In the US, we Somalis are called Somali Americans. This means we need to take the best components of both cultures. Many Somalis may move to the US, learn English, get a job, buy a new car, and rent a new apartment, but they usually do not want to abandon their language, religious practices, and ancestral culture."[8] Many Somalis I interviewed said they combined their identities as both Somalis and Americans.

"My three kids were born in the US," said one mother. "I want them to be fully American without forgetting their roots. I want them to keep our Somali traditions and language and pass them to their children and grandchildren as much as they can. We are not opposed to the American culture. We really embrace it without abandoning ours. I want my children to celebrate Fourth of July and Somali independence at the same time. I want them to continue to respect both cultures simultaneously but to be always mindful of who they are."

The discussion of assimilation and integration requires us to look more closely at American cultural values and norms, how widely held they are among Americans, and how different they are from Somali cultural values and norms. American culture is not homogeneous, and cultural values and norms are held by various people to varying degrees. The term *culture wars* captures the sometimes acrimonious differences in values and norms. Americans disagree on cultural value issues such as the right to abortion, gay marriage, the role of religion in politics, the role of government in society, individualism versus communitarianism, rights versus responsibilities, and so on. Similarly, the cultural values held by many Somalis are also held by many Americans: the importance of hard work and responsibility; the importance of family, faith, and community; the need for moral responsibility; the spirit of entrepreneurship; the importance of education; and so on. Therefore, whenever we discuss assimilation and integration, we need to remember the heterogeneity of American culture and the similar cultural values and norms that many Americans and Somalis hold. A good question for dialogue is: What are those similarities? There are more than one might think.

What Does It Mean to be *American*?

The questions "What does it mean to be an American?" and "Who can become an American?" are not always easy to answer. In general terms, Americans have never fully agreed on what it means to be an American. Abdi Mahad explained what it means to him:

Being American is more than simply having been born in the US. I think people don't need to be white to be fully American, a US citizen. I believe there's no distinction between born and naturalized citizens. I've met a few white Americans who think US-born white Americans are "more" American than naturalized citizens, which is not accurate. Becoming an American citizen does not come to us so easily. One thing we have to do is to learn the answers to one hundred civic questions by heart; I don't think most US-born citizens can even pass such a test. We all have sworn to defend and die for the Constitution, an oath that natural-born citizens usually don't take. Once you have American citizenship, you are an American.

For me, being an American means being tolerant of all the different ethnicities, races, religions, and cultures. Being American is to be able to express your ideas and beliefs without an iota of fear, prejudice, and blind generalization. Being American is to respect each other's cultures and treat everyone equally regardless of our differences. Being an American means that we are all treated equally, no matter what color skin you have, no matter what religion or culture you are from.

We must be aware that we all have come here from so many places with so many different backgrounds. I believe no culture is superior to others. Therefore, immigrants and refugees must not be forced to conform to certain expectations of the dominant society. I don't think the US has one common culture to which everyone can cling. Being an American means that you are free to pursue your life, vote for who you want to, and travel around anywhere in the US without fear of being randomly searched, harassed, harangued, and followed around.[9]

I asked interviewees who varied in English language proficiency, educational level, socioeconomic status, and years in the United States if they identified as a Somali American, American, or African American. Most said that they wanted to be labeled as Somali American. They said they could be Americans who express their devotion to their new country and retain their distinctive identities without abolishing their heritage. Somalis have become proud, loyal, and contributing Americans, but they do not intend to lose their own ethnic identity in the melting pot. Unlike some European countries, where one must fully assimilate to be a citizen, in the United States, one can maintain his or her unique cultural identity and be an American citizen.

During my interviews, I learned that Somali people may have some confusion as to who they are. Many Somalis have divided-heart syndrome. These people may say,

"America is my new country, but my heart lies in my home-land." Some other Somalis repudiate their own ancestral culture and adopt the larger society's cultures. This group forsakes anything that is related to their Somali cultural identities like food, clothes, and music. Others discard and disassociate themselves from their native culture and refuse to assimilate into the host community. This latter group avoids calling themselves Somalis or Americans. Some older Somalis do not really want to integrate or assimilate; they want to return to Somalia as soon as it is safe to do so.

Barriers of the First-Generation Somalis

I am often asked if Somalis are ready to assimilate. White assimilationists may superficially understand Somalis' reluctance to integrate or assimilate into the mainstream culture but know little about barriers hindering the process. What are the challenges that limit or reduce the likelihood of integration or assimilation? Are current integration and assimilation processes much different from those that prevailed in earlier times?

Language and Culture Barriers

Saint Cloud's Somali population is overwhelmingly comprised of new arrivals from East Africa, an area with considerably more diverse languages and cultures than Minnesota. My interviewees argued that having a common culture and language facilitates communication and inter-action among recent Somali arrivals in the United States and central Minnesota. "Most recent Somalis who came to the US with no or limited English language skills have clearly faced numerous challenges that impede them from integrating into the American way of life," said Ahmed Ali, a lead staff organizer at the Greater Minnesota Worker Center, Saint Cloud. "Integration means understanding the culture of other people fully. The best way to understand the dominant American culture is to learn English. Speaking English is an essential component for most people living in the US. When immigrants and refugees do not know English well, their ability to find jobs or socialize with others will be minimal."[10] Therefore, lack of English language and cultural knowledge is the most formidable barrier for Somalis in Saint Cloud and its environs, limiting employment, education, and slowing the improvement of their socioeconomic status.

Language is not the only barrier hindering Somalis' ability to integrate. I often see Somalis who have gained English competency remain emotionally attached to their language and culture. This means the acquisition of English does not necessarily lead to a total integration. "Even though proficiency in the English language is an important component for integration, cultural knowledge of the host community is essential," said Abdirizak Jama, a patient care extender.[11]

Residential Concentration

Many white friends wonder why Somalis live in areas largely, if not exclusively, populated by their tight-knit ethnic community. Several factors lead Somalis to settle in these places. Many Somalis say they feel most at home in their own ethnic communities, around people from their culture and faith. They can find stores that sell their ethnic food and garb. They also have mosques in their neighborhoods. Some tell me the cost of living in their neighborhoods is inexpensive compared to many white areas and the suburbs. Some others say they can retain their ancestral heritage, language, and customs more easily in their Somali-populated locations. Abdi Mahad argued:

> Somalis' residential concentration in the urban neighborhoods is strongly related to socioeconomic inequality. Not all Somalis are white collar, college educated. These low-income Somalis can't afford to live in some areas in the city. I believe the place of residence plays a crucial role in encouraging mutual

interaction between the late-arriving refugees and longtime residents. Irrespective of years of residence, any type of residential concentration delays or limits Somalis from fully integrating into the society of which they have become a part. When new refugees live in concentrated communities where a large percent of the residents were born in their native land, they may well be less integrated, in terms of academic, economic, and civic integration. However, this is not necessarily the case since one can go from their tight-knit community to work, school, the Walmart store, and so on, and interact with members of the broader community. However, those new refugees are probably less likely to be fluent in English if they only speak Somali in their neighborhood.[12]

Many Somalis agree that residential concentration provides limited incentive to learn the English language and American customs. Some scholars, however, believe such ethnic concentration has important positive bonding and support functions for members of an immigrant or refugee group, and may slow down integration but not block it. Geographic relocation may come more comfortably for the second generation of Somali residents.

Length of Time in Residence

Historically, different immigrant and refugee groups have taken distinct paths to integration depending upon the time period; their reasons for resettlement, such as war or economic factors; how similar the country they left was to the United States; the openness of the host community; the skill set of the immigrants; if they had friends and family in the new country; and so on. For instance, Scandinavians, Germans, Italians, and European Jews from Germany and Austria fleeing persecution did not have the same integration process. The Irish probably integrated sooner than Germans and Italians because they spoke English and were familiar with British culture. Somalis who lived in Kenya have an easier time integrating than Somalis from Somalia or Ethiopia because many of them speak English and there are more aspects of American culture in Kenya.

Many of the Somalis I interviewed think the process of integration is related to how long one lives in the United States. They claim that Somalis residing in the United States for a long time will display greater similarities with their host community than will recent Somali arrivals. "No wave of earlier European immigrants has assimilated into the mainstream society immediately upon arrival," observed Abdi Mahad. "Germans, Scandinavians, and other Europeans who immigrated to Minnesota kept their culture and languages for decades. Somalis are no different from those early European immigrants who retained their customs as much as they could." Some citizens of European descent still celebrate their distinctive cultures and characteristics with parades, food festivals, musical performances, sporting events, and speaking their ancestors' tongue.

In central Minnesota, many Somalis are new to the country. "Somali parents in Saint Cloud are not that old, and their children born outside of America as well are too young to integrate," said Abdirahim Osman, a businessman. "A full degree of integration will take time. This means complete linguistic, economic, and cultural integration depends on the length of time the Somalis stay in the US."[13]

"I don't think full integration has a fixed timetable," said Abdi Daisane of Resource Inc. Employment Action Center. "The complete degree and process of economic success hinges on the familiarity with the language and culture of the host society of which we are a part."[14]

Even though I agree that living in the United States for a long time helps immigrants and refugees familiarize themselves with English, not all Somalis face the same barriers to integration. Somalis with urban backgrounds are more likely than Somalis with rural backgrounds to integrate into American society easily and quickly because urban areas in East Africa are cosmopolitan to various degrees and have similarities with urban areas in the United States. Cities like Nairobi are "world cities" and in many ways are more cosmopolitan than Saint Cloud, resembling such international cities as New York or London.

Amount of interaction with non-Somalis, itself an indicator of integration, also helps with further integration. "Somalis' integration in the Twin Cities is faster than Somalis' integration in Saint Cloud," reported Ahmed Ali. "Somalis in the Twin Cities tend to move around and interact with non-Somali communities." Factors like length of time in residence do play an important role in integration. Factors like the country one comes from play an important role too.

Racism and Nativism

Every time a new wave of immigrants or refugees arrives, some people, for various reasons, have negative sentiments about them. I find most Saint Cloud–born white residents welcoming, tolerant, friendly, and accepting. While some Somalis have experienced prejudice and discrimination in Saint Cloud, the 2015 *Social Capital Survey: Central Minnesota* reported that the level of the host community's trust of Somalis had actually risen from 56 percent to 73 percent during the 2010 to 2015 period.[15] Historically, it might be worth remembering that Germans, Jews, Italians, Irish, and Southeast Asians were greeted with derision by some host community members when they first arrived. Therefore, what is the connection between integration and Somalis' experience with prejudice?

As I noted earlier, Somalis actually have many cultural values that are similar to those held by the people of central Minnesota. However, distinctive in their traditionally worn veils, some Somalis have experienced hostility. Many late-arriving Somalis with whom I spoke said they felt they did not belong to the community to which they came for safety and refuge. Some said that they faced challenges in gaining acceptance at work and school. Because of the prejudice they've experienced, some Somalis show a resistance to integrate into the broader American society. Instead, they choose to live among their ethnic communities and continue to preserve their culture. "Both overt and subtle discrimination limiting equal employment opportunities hamper a comprehensive integration," said Ahmed Ali. "Negative experiences of Somalis slow down the rate of integration. Integration happens when people feel welcome and accepted. Because of the rising prejudice, even law-abiding Somali American citizens who are educated may feel like they are nothing but aliens."[16]

"Integration is like when I come to your home as a first-time guest and you either welcome me in or refuse to see me," said a community elder who wanted to remain anonymous. "When I feel unwanted, excluded, and unvalued, my ethnic consciousness and deep affection for my culture will be more exclusively stronger than ever. The exclusion, lack of sense of belonging, and lack of equal opportunities will negatively impact integration. My exposure to mainstream American culture will definitely be marginal." Discrimination has reduced the opportunities for some Somalis to integrate. A few Somali college graduates with highly employable skills stated that they think the main obstacles blocking integration are not just language and cultural familiarity but also Somali ethnicity.

During my interviews, I found that first-generation Somalis seem to face more prejudice and discrimination than their second-generation children, who do not have a strange accent and adapt well to American culture because they have a better understanding of that culture. Part of the reason for their acceptance is that the second generation feels and acts more Americanized than their parents.

Integration requires that recently arrived immigrants and refugees are assisted in their transition into the local American community. Offering the new arrivals equal working and economic opportunities is the foundation of successful integration. Tolerance and respect of the rights of refugees and immigrants is also a crucial precondition for successful integration.

Social and Economic Inequalities

After leaving behind civil war and strife in their home country, Somalis arrive optimistic at the prospect of moving up the socioeconomic ladder. Each new immigrant attempts to take full advantage of the American Dream. When examining how well Somalis have settled into mainstream American society, it is important to measure the extent of economic integration and their current socioeconomic status. Are they contributing to the society economically? Are they creating jobs? Do they have higher education, and do they purchase homes?

Sadly, many Somalis in Saint Cloud and its environs work in relatively lower-paying entry-level jobs, compared to members of the host community. One community elder said, "Even though there are a number of low-income whites in this area with low-paying jobs, on average there is a stark difference in wages between Somalis and established residents. Therefore, the existing socioeconomic factors, such as education and income, have generated some disparity." According to Minnesota state government statistics on income, Somalis are the poorest group in Minnesota.[17]

After having interviewed many Somalis, both those with a lot of education and a little, I found that there was a sizeable wage gap among Somalis themselves. Those who have postsecondary education and fluent language skills fare better than late-arriving Somalis with limited education and English-language skills. The reason new arrivals experience less economic integration is that they don't have the language proficiency and human capital that may be specifically needed in the American labor market.

Because of the lack of available jobs for many Somali college graduates, many choose to leave Saint Cloud to look for employment in other cities and states. Some Somalis argue that there simply are not enough jobs in the Saint Cloud area for college grads. They may end up taking jobs that do not require a college education. For example, two of my close friends who graduated from St. Cloud State University became taxi drivers in Chicago. Some others took poor-paying jobs in the Twin Cities, while a few who chose to stay in the Saint Cloud area became cultural navigators in Apollo and Tech High Schools. Many other graduates open their own businesses, such as grocery stores, coffee shops, restaurants, and tax return agencies, or start nonprofit organizations. Somalis in Saint Cloud, whether they have a college or high school degree, face obstacles to economic integration. Because of barriers that all Somalis face, only a few college graduates have had the opportunity to make an impact on their community.

Some of the problems Somali college graduates are facing may well be problems all college graduates in central Minnesota face. I see many CSB/SJU and SCSU grads leave central Minnesota to seek jobs elsewhere. If there is a structural deficit in college-graduate-level jobs, then employment centers and nonprofit organizations in the area should be working to help create higher-level jobs that can utilize college-educated workers. This would also be good for the local economy. One community elder who preferred not to have his name mentioned in the book said:

> I think the situation of Somali graduates can't be equated with non-Somali college graduates. Young non-Somali college graduates want something exhilarating and entertaining that encompasses a lot of diversity, so they love to move to major metropolitan areas, while Somali college graduates move to the cities just because no one hires them for jobs that correspond with their educational level.

"To me, integration means working," said Ahmed Ali. "We Somalis are working. We are contributing to the society of which we are a part. Those among us who have a hard time finding employment have not yet integrated very well. I see joblessness as a conspicuous barrier that's slowing down the process of integration." Employment not only contributes to overall integration and participation in the broader community by providing income and social connections, it is also an important form of integration in itself.

A limited ability to speak English is not the only barrier. Income disparities, poor educational attainment, lack of civic participation, and many more factors retard the pace of integration. Most Somalis encounter challenges as they struggle to adapt to Minnesota life. Most families with rural backgrounds told me they experienced conflicting feelings when they arrived, and they had difficulties navigating foreign things like culture, food, and weather. The combination of trauma born of the civil war or current violence back home, their displacement experiences, and the loss of loved ones has also triggered psychological conditions, such as anxiety, depression, and post-traumatic stress, impacting Somalis' overall propensity to integrate.

Bonding and Bridging

I asked members of the Somali community about different topics related to integration. Many Somalis told me they are stuck at the lowest rung of the occupational, educational, and income ladder. To survive in their new home and overcome their daily challenges, most Somalis have a strong bonding social capital. "Bonding social capital is an advantage to lower-income families whose livelihood depends on their deep attachment to their clan support system," said Abdi Mahad. "Somalis band together as a means of survival. Within their concentrated communities, each Somali finds a clan support network that helps them to overcome challenges and build new lives." Yet the structure of Somali clans may hinder integration and adaptation. During my interviews, I found that some Somalis demonstrated reluctance to engage outside their communities. If a clan demands steadfast loyalty and commitment, bonding activity within the group makes it more difficult for the individual to "bridge" or integrate with others outside the group. However, many young Somalis are more likely to rely on their education than their clan membership. Mariam Ali, a twenty-nine-year-old university student, believes that bonding should not hamper Somalis' efforts to economically, academically, and socially integrate into their host communities. Mariam explained:

> A clan is a part of our everyday life. We hear someone belongs to that clan or this clan. We use *clan* to describe someone's roots every day, but there is a line between identifying with a clan and being clannish. Yes, I belong to a certain clan, but I don't believe that my clan or someone else's clan is superior to others. I will not treat a person or group of people

differently based on their clan origin. For many, I think it's impossible to separate one from the other. The question is, why do some Somalis more than others cling to clan loyalty? To answer this, I need to look at it from different perspectives.

First, unresolved clan grievances, political divisions, and tensions in Somalia lead to overt social cleavages, competition, and hatred among various clan members living in central Minnesota. Most of us still consider clan loyalty as an integral part of Somali society. It also influences all aspects of Somali life. Most cities in the US are identified with some specific clans. Within their ethnic neighborhoods, some clan members cluster together in an area more than other Somali clan members. When new refugees are resettled in locations where their kinsfolk are scarce, the new arrivals move to areas near their clan compatriots. This type of "neighborhood clanization" leads to an abrupt chain-migration pattern. I meet a lot of recently arrived Somalis who think they can't survive as individuals outside of their particular neighborhoods. They also believe they can better keep their own heritage and customs alive when they congregate in the same neighborhoods.

I don't want to demonize the Somali clan system. I witness people seeking assistance from their fellow clan members. For me, I don't see any problem with settling near the people who you know well. We don't have to move out of our Somali neighborhoods to integrate into white America.

Among the youth, it is interesting to see that the clan structure is not important in all of their lives. Rahma Abdi, a nineteen-year-old college student, said:

> None of my close friends belongs to my sub-clan. Our Somali youth today do not have to rely on clan loyalty like our parents and grandparents do. We are not anything like the older generation. I think the older people may have experienced conflict. Some saw their family members killed, tortured, or gang-raped in front of them. Such negative experiences can be one of the reasons older adults tend to be more attached to clans than young people are. I think part of their deep-seated clan loyalty is just the fact that they were raised in a different time. It mostly stems from the environment they grew up in. I think they can't let go of wrongs that have been done to them. Sometimes people who are close to you force you to make friends

with or date someone who shares a similar clan background with you. I believe it is not wrong to know
someone's clan, but it's very wrong to discriminate
against someone just because of his or her clan group-
ing. Everyone should be treated with respect.

Sumio Abdi, a twenty-five-year-old woman, also thinks
clan attachment is not as important for the younger generation as it is for older Somalis:

Young people couldn't care less about what clan one
belongs to. My close friends come from different clans.
The clique we form is always based on our locality
and neighborhood. We are not like our older people,
who have a hard time understanding the difference
between clan and clannism. Everyone belongs to a
clan, and that is not bad. What is wrong is if we
discriminate against each other based on our clan
affiliations, which is clannism. If we hate each other,
we hang on to clannish tendencies. Our Islamic religion ordains us to use clans to know each other, but
not to discriminate against each other. Some of the
positive aspects of using clans include mutual assistance and support in the difficult times. When new
Somali people come to the US, neighbors welcome

them and help them acclimate to the new system. When a member of their family gets sick, arrested, or laid off, the clan becomes the only support system available for them. A negative aspect of deep adherence to one's clan is that it leads to extreme bonding social capital, and excessive bonding is believed to restrict economic and social opportunities for us to integrate into our host community.

Generation Gap

The relationship between the younger and older generations of Somalis in central Minnesota is weakening. The more I interviewed Somalis, the more I learned of tensions developing between parents and their children. Once Somalis settle in the United States, young people acclimatize and integrate into the host community faster than their older Somali parents and grandparents who keep their traditional way of life. Ali Abdi, a sixty-seven-year-old grandpa, complained about lack of good interaction with his grandkids. He said:

> Now I live with my grandkids. Guess what, we can't agree on a simple thing, like food, dating, preservation of our ancestral heritage, and so on. For example, I enjoy home-cooked Somali food; they eat

hamburgers and so many other types of food that I can't even name them all now. I recommend that they listen to the Quran, but rap music is blaring every day. I urge them to keep their cultural identity intact, but they tell me they have integrated themselves into mainstream US society. The younger generation often feels more "American" than "Somali," and they grow up surrounded by friends and classmates who are not Somalis. I don't have issues with that, but my issue is that they avoid holding on to the cultural practices of their parents and grandparents, and they instead become more Americanized as they grow up in the US. When you lose your culture, you lose your identity and integrity. They idolize and admire athletes, movie stars, and rappers more than their parents and grandparents. They sit in a corner and read books while they forget their unique and deep-rooted family traditions and stories.

Khadija, a mother of four, thinks she and her kids don't see eye to eye:

I don't think I can even talk to my son. He is always mad at something. As a mom, I try to talk to him about how his day at school went. I feel like we have a high wall with a coiled barbed wire between us. Back home, we had strong parent-child ties. Deep down, the children who were born or grew up in the United States think they are smarter than their parents. They think they are independent and free to do whatever they want to do. I think one reason that widens the gap between Somali-born parents and their American-born kids is that our kids take on adult responsibilities at an early age because their parents are illiterate. The kids help us interpret, read our mail, and answer our phones.

Ibado Haji is a twenty-nine-year-old mother who believes she has learned how to maintain a balanced sense of Somali American identity without furthering the chasm between the generations:

Some Somali parents like me are unnecessarily strict with our kids. We tend to forget, or maybe we are not aware, that they are struggling with their dual identity. Our kids are so confused as to who they are. Many times, my kids asked me who they were. Every time I ask them, "What do you think?" they say, "I think we are Americans." Sometime I see my kids being critical of our Somali way of dressing and cooking. My younger daughter came up to me with something that looked like our Somali *mal-awah*, crepes. She told me it was called *lefse*. She taught me how to bake it. To make her happy, I bake her lefse, because she has already refused to eat our homemade crepes. At home, she's bossing everyone around, and I can say that "she becomes the tail that wags the dog." I believe if our kids are willing to become a part of the American culture, then let's allow them to do so.

Younger Somali kids perceive dependence on the family and the clan support system as a major hindrance to their success in the host community. I have seen American-born kids prefer freedom or individuality to community and clan attachment. Halima, a mother of six, believes the Somali kids' disobedience comes from their sense of independence and individuality:

As soon as we came to the US, our children started going to school while we worked for them in many low-paying shifts. All we do is sacrifice to help them to succeed in school. Our children help us interpret. Now our role at home is demoted. The kids are the ones who answer the phone, read our mail for us, make or cancel a hospital appointment.

Because we depend on them, some began rebelling against our ideas or orders.

Aisha, an eighteen-year-old girl who studies art education, recalled when her parents objected to her desire to sketch human and animal figures:

My family came to Minnesota when I was three years old. When I was ten years old, I sketched some images of people and animals. My dad snatched the paper from my hand and tore it to pieces. I had no idea why he did it. I looked up at him and I saw his face full of rage, his finger wiggling at me angrily. My eyes widened in shock. Some tears welled up in my eyes. "You can't draw anything else, okay?" Dad threatened. His words hurt my feelings because I always loved to be an artist. No matter what my dad said, I never lost my passion to sketch and draw things. I continued sketching without the knowledge of my parents. A few days after, I asked a Somali school navigator if there were some restrictions for Muslim students in art class. She said to me, "We, Somali Muslims, cannot illustrate, paint, or sculpt any living thing." She advised me to concentrate on drawing floral leaf patterns and other nonliving beings. Now, I am going to an art school.

Even though there is a generation gap, most Somali parents want their kids to succeed in school so they will achieve the American Dream that they themselves have not been able to. Some Somalis told me about the difficult sacrifices their families made for them. Abdi Daisane, who recently ran for Saint Cloud City Council, said:

> My parents encouraged me to pursue a higher education. Particularly, my dad told me to focus on education rather than working. My parents instilled in me the importance of education and of work for the community. Sometimes we fail to appreciate how strong our parents are and the sacrifices they are making to see their kids be successful in school and in life. Within a short time, I achieved a lot. This shows us how our parents' commitment to helping us works. The level of educational accomplishment, political immersion, and economic contribution to our new country prove to be significant.

Ummu Abdi, a twenty-two-year-old college student, is grateful to her parents for her education:

My mom did all she could to help me. She has always been there for me. I know our parents, regardless of their past education and poor English language skill, want the best for their children. They work in multiple shifts to raise us better, encourage us to get the best education and a job. They don't complain how hard their work is. They don't grumble about the calluses on their hands. All they want is to see us be successful and productive.

Similarly, Sumio Abdi, a twenty-five-year-old, believes her mom did all she could to encourage her education:

My dad died a long time ago, and my mom plays a dual role in our family. She works in multiple shifts to make sure we stay in school and focus on our education more than anything else. She encourages me to complete my education and accomplish my academic goals. Most Somali parents I meet do not have much education, but they are committed to doing all they can to see their kids succeed in school. Because of language barriers, some parents do not know whether their kids are progressing or falling behind in school. Sadly, our parents can't figure out whether we need more support at school or not.

These sacrifices show how much effort Somali parents make for their children to succeed and to integrate into America.

Nostalgia

The older generation with their limited education and English skills, like my grandma Mariam, do not want to integrate. They hang on to the hope that they will return to their country of origin when the violence comes to an end. Despite the fact that she lives with her daughters and her grandchildren, my grandmother says she feels lonely and pesters me to return her back home. Somali seniors face physical and psychological isolation and stress. Older Somalis have nostalgia for Africa and want to go back. "The older generation doesn't socialize outside of the home as much as the younger generations do," said Mohamoud Ali, a community elder. Ali continued:

> As soon as older people come to America, they begin missing things they knew in Somalia. Some feel a mixture of emotions. For them, leaving behind their loved ones and relatives has led them to live in a baffling state. Our young children and grandchildren knew from the day they arrived that they were expected to become "good Americans."

That meant learning English and accepting it as the national tongue. It meant getting a job and being productive members of society. For older folks, integration does not work. So, I am comfortable to live in my home country where I don't have to beg others for an interpretation. I'd love to go to a country where I am familiar with the language, culture, weather, and rules.

Second Generation

Regardless of older Somalis' strong rejection of some aspects of assimilation, younger Somali Americans are integrating quickly into the mainstream American community, just like the second generation of the earliest European immigrants. Second-generation children are understandably more likely to perceive themselves as more American than their foreign-born parents. They have a deeper attachment to the United States.

Today, the vast majority of Somali refugees' children are becoming fluent in English while simultaneously losing the ability to speak their parents' languages. During my interviews, I found that many bilingual children preferred to speak English rather than Somali, their mother tongue, at home. It is wrong to assume Somalis are not integrating in terms of education and language proficiency.

Many young American-born children with refugee parents now find themselves disconnected from the traditions of their parents to varying degrees. They feel they have more freedom to dress like, date, or marry those outside of their ethnicity and religion than previous generations have. Some interviewees debated whether or not intermarriage is one of the outcomes of the melting pot process.

Today, Somali youth learn English quickly and integrate into American society because they go to school and have diverse schoolmates and colleagues. Today, young Somalis "make up roughly 20 percent of the total student enrollment in Saint Cloud local middle and high schools."[18]

"American-born children of Somali parents will have better advancement in terms of acquisition of college education, entry into the workforce, and municipal positions in the near future," said Abdirizak Jama, a college student and patient care extender. "These growing generations will, one day soon, become more similar to natives over time by acquiring local human capital. Unlike their foreign-born parents, the second or third generation will achieve full social and economic integration."[19] Many second-generation Somalis tell me they tend to catch on quickly and may even do better than natives one day.

Civic Integration

Many Somalis aspire to climb the political ladder. For them, any political participation, by definition, means becoming involved in local American practices like voting and caucusing. Although American politics is new to Somalis, a few individuals have chosen to run for office in Saint Cloud and its environs. Like central Minnesota-born American residents, Somalis are involved in political campaigns, donate to their desired political parties and candidates, and sign petitions to their local, state, and national politicians.

In Saint Cloud, Abdul Kulane, a graduate of Saint John's University, competed with Dave Masters and Darrell Bruestle for Ward 1 representative to the city council in 2014. He was the first Somali American in Saint Cloud to run for such a position. Even though Abdul did not win to become a Saint Cloud City council member, his effort ignited passion and ambition among young Somalis in the city. Several Somali Americans in Saint Cloud also ran for the District 742 school board. Abdi Daisane, a twenty-eight-year-old Somali American man who graduated from St. Cloud State University, also ran for a city council seat. "When Somali Americans get involved in American politics, they tend to focus on advocating for better education, creating better opportunities for all residents in Saint Cloud," said Daisane.

What Does Saint Cloud Do for You?

At the end of the general election in November 2016, I interviewed a couple of Somali Americans in Saint Cloud who were appreciative of and grateful to their city for all the opportunities they've received.

Abdi Daisane said:

> Even though I came to the US seven years ago, I feel like I achieved a lot. Upon my arrival to Saint Cloud, I went to school. Fortunately, I found respectable educators and mentors who were committed to helping me be successful. Those right mentors are likely to show you the way if you are willing to work to learn. When I was a student at my former college in Nebraska, where I was the only Somali, I did not have the support needed to get ahead in education, neither did I have the right mentors willing to help me. In Saint Cloud, I felt a sense of belonging. In our city, I see many college students who look like me, and the support I received emboldened me to focus on my education. I started becoming involved in campus and became a member of student government and other clubs. I got a degree in planning and community development from St. Cloud State University. Apart from the support at the

university, the Somali community and city officials also are part of the reason for my success and education. I mean, Saint Cloud offered me education for which I am thankful. I consider it as the proper environment for someone like me to succeed and become part of the larger community.

I grew up in a refugee camp in Kenya for over eighteen years. So, I ask myself, "What would my life have been like if I had never come to Saint Cloud?" If I had remained at the refugee camp, I would possibly have lived my whole life within a few miles' radius of where I grew up. I know if I were there, I would not have completed even high school. And no one would have helped me thrive in the world.

I am grateful to Saint Cloud for giving me this opportunity to study and run for Saint Cloud City Council in 2016. The community and its officials create a ladder for people to climb to success, regardless of skin color and faith. I strongly believe anyone can reach his or her potential if they play by the rules. I feel I accomplished my American Dream like other refugees and immigrants before me. Today, I am helping other Somalis with their dreams and aspirations to be part of our great community. I give the gift of education and mentorship to those around me. Our host community loves the determination and drive Somalis show in the pursuit of success.[20]

Farhiyo Idifle, a thirty-one-year-old woman, said:

I came to the US in 2007 from Hagerdera refugee camp. At the refugee camp, I completed high school. As soon as I came to Saint Cloud, I went to St. Cloud Technical and Community College right away and pursued higher education. I did not want to stay home. All I wanted was to get an education and reach my American Dream. I have a BA and MS of social work. I am a licensed graduate social worker. I am now working at a Stearns Benton Employment Training Council as a career planner. Saint Cloud provided me education and employment. I am grateful to the city of Saint Cloud for their welcoming. Saint Cloud is a great place to live, work, and raise families. So far, I have discovered that people living in our city are friendly and communicative. People from our host community that I meet want to learn much from us if we communicate effectively with them. Some are very curious about our refugee journey, barriers we met, and how we overcame them. I like people who like to know more about our culture, traditions, and our ethnic food.

Can Somalis Vote?

On Election Day, November 8, 2016, I saw a man harassing a young Somali woman at a polling place in Saint Cloud. I overheard him say, "You are an illegal immigrant, and you can't vote." I approached the man peacefully and told him that under federal law, only noncitizens could not vote in a presidential election. In 2012, I was on a DFL campaign when a white woman approached me and asked me if Somalis could vote for any party. I explained to her that naturalized US citizens have the same voting rights as natural-born citizens and that those naturalized US citizens can cast a ballot for whomever they wish. Once a Somali person passes the citizenship test and takes the Oath of Allegiance, he or she can get US citizenship, gain the right to vote, and run for and hold any elected government positions, except for US president.

At present, it appears that most Somali Americans identify themselves as Democrats, while a few support the Republican Party. Regardless of their party affiliations, both Democratic and Republican parties approach Somali Americans for support and votes. Abdi Mahad observed:

Even though many Somalis may not have much exposure to local politics, some older Somalis I talk to confide in me that they primarily lean towards the Republican Party's conservative values, and they are diametrically opposed to some of the positions of the Democratic Party on social issues such as abortion, legalization of same sex marriage, funding Planned Parenthood, and many other issues. Despite the views some Somalis have on social issues, many Somalis vote for the Democratic Party. Somalis argue that the Democratic Party has stood up for lower- and middle-class families, more freedom, Medicare, and Social Security. They also believe the Republican Party does not support equal opportunity for all in terms of education, employment, and affordable health care, and are religiously intolerant, anti-Muslim, anti-immigrant, and anti-refugee, among other things. I think Republican candidates in central Minnesota don't devote much time and attention to the issues that matter to Somalis, but Democratic Party candidates mobilize politically underrepresented and potential Somali voters.[21]

Regardless of the parties' different political platforms, candidates frequent locations where there's a heavy concentration of the Somali population in order to gain their support. Omar Podi, an active DFL organizer who worked in New Haven, Connecticut, and Saint Louis, Missouri, before he moved to Saint Cloud on June 12, 2012, explained how the DFL state party reaches out to potential Somali American voters living in central Minnesota to garner their votes. "Saint Cloud–area candidates often focus on reaching out to their registered voters," said Podi. "They meet with Somali community members and attend Somali community meetings often as a strategy to draw in higher participation of voters. Somali Americans themselves reach out to their potential candidates. The DFL invites them to speak at our meetings."[22] I personally saw Saint Cloud–area DFL candidates mobilize Somali voters at Somali shopping malls, city parks, public events, and mosques.

I assisted Somali voters with limited English skills.

The Somali American population is growing in central Minnesota, but Somali voter turnout still lacks momentum. Some Somalis say the candidates who reach out to them do not understand the problems they are facing. There are some barriers confronting Saint Cloud–area Somali Americans when trying to vote. Most Somali Americans whom I met work in multiple shifts and have families for which they must care. Some clearly said they had no time to vote. Some others said that no one has ever effectively informed them about issues related to voting and the names of candidates who were willing to support them. Assisting eligible Somali American community members to register and vote may require a lot of work. Omar Podi, the tireless DFL organizer, said:

> Most Somali Americans who are eligible to register and vote are unaware of the names of the candidates and their voting precincts. I think the person's level of education and socioeconomic status are factors that influence who votes. Sometimes familiarity with the American voting system is important. I also see people who are educated but are unwilling to vote for any party. Since Somali Americans in the Saint Cloud area are new voters, I do all I can

to educate them about how voting works. I explain to them who each candidate is and what each says he or she will do if elected. Sometimes I show them some mock ballot papers to help them become acquainted with the voting system.

In the Saint Cloud area, I estimate that 20 percent of the Somali people are politically involved in voting while 80 percent are in the process of learning about voting. Each time I talk to some members of the Somali community in the Saint Cloud area, many have perceptions that voting made no difference in the past. Some outright resisted voting at all. Whenever I meet them, I explain to them that they need to exercise their fundamental right to vote. I also tell them that they can influence who gets elected if they turn out in groups to vote. Most of these voters are Somali-born and have language barriers. I often tell these eligible voters they have their rights as voters to have access to an interpreter at the polling stations.

With social media, reaching out to prospective Somali American voters is not that difficult. When communicating with my fellow Saint Cloud–area Somali American voters, they tell me they care about things like subsidized and affordable housing and health care, but the most common complaints I hear include poor housing, unemployment, and lack of business expansion. The Somali community wants to have their long-standing problems resolved once and for all.

After having seen the importance of canvassing and engaging voters to participate in the voting process, I held numerous voter education forums to educate and mobilize the Saint Cloud–area Somali Americans to increase the voter turnout. Despite the existing skepticism, our outreach at the voter empowerment and education gatherings in central Minnesota bore fruit. After holding these civic engagement activities and volunteer phone calls, the Saint Cloud–area Somali American community became civically engaged. I registered 7,042 Somali Americans who were eligible to vote in Saint Cloud and Waite Park. Today, most Somalis are aware of who is on their side.

Younger Somali Americans have far higher expectations than their parents do about becoming involved in local politics. The Millennials have a deeper attachment to US politics than they do to politics back home in Somalia. Some came out to knock on doors with their favorite candidates.[23]

During the elections, I witnessed Podi and his team arranging transportation to and from a voting site. They reminded Somali American voters of the location of their local polling place. Many new voters walked out of the polling stations feeling empowered.

Conclusion

Integration is a method in which a minority group becomes involved in the economy by getting a job, an education, opening a business, or becoming involved politically by voting or running for political office. Such integration depends on English language proficiency and acquisition of citizenship. These are particularly significant for Somalis' success in their new society. Allowing recent Somali arrivals to enjoy equal rights in employment and educational opportunities is also critical to integration. Better education will help immigrants attain higher advanced degrees that will allow them access to high-wage employment and better housing. Somalis who insulate themselves in their own ethnic neighborhoods should be aware that they arrived in a country where opportunities for everyone are available if they pursue education and develop English language proficiency. After having talked to many Somalis, I have learned that integration takes time and occurs when Somalis have full access to opportunities comparable to those available to individuals in the host society.

Saint Cloud city officials should develop a new political framework for engaging recently arrived foreign-born groups. An encouraging foundation for such a framework is the results of the 2015 *Social Capital Survey*, which found that 74 percent of the host community members trusted Somalis. To become more familiar with each other, both native-born residents and Somalis should interact more in planned, structured ways, such as Circles of Understanding (a program in which diverse members of the Saint Cloud community get to know each other) and joint community projects. Longtime residents of Saint Cloud should welcome immigrants and refugees and help them develop a sense of belonging so they can partake in all aspects of social, academic, cultural, and economic life. All barriers and misconceptions must be removed. This is the American way at its best.

Chapter 5

BUSINESS

You will never profit from bended knees.

—Somali proverb

Unlike many immigrants, Somali refugees had nothing in their possession when they arrived in Minnesota but the hope of rebuilding their shattered lives from scratch. To earn their living, they worked very hard over multiple shifts in various entry-level jobs requiring little English. Their work was fatiguing, and new arrivals earned meager salaries. A few Somalis who had operated businesses in Somalia decided to work independently in their new country by opening stores selling ethnic food and clothing. Some with no prior business experience also opened businesses.

In 2000, there was no substantial number of Somali businesses to speak of in Saint Cloud. Today, a large and growing percentage of local business is Somali-owned. Every month, new businesses open their doors to the Saint Cloud community, including those restaurants, clothing shops, and grocery stores looking for more consumers.

"Somali entrepreneurship makes a tangible contribution to the local and US economy," said Tohow Siyad, a business owner. "In order to sustain their growth, it is crucial to reduce the high rate of unemployment in minority communities, to provide investment and capital access for minority-owned businesses."

It is important to examine how immigration causes expansion in self-employment that accelerates improvement in labor market conditions. Sadly, most contemporary research on smaller businesses has focused on the traditional models of ownership, overlooking or misunderstanding Somali American entrepreneurs' constraints and role in the economy. Therefore, the purpose of this chapter is to explain the economic contribution of Somali entrepreneurs, identify the numerous challenges small-business owners in Saint Cloud face, and present an alternative to the existing problem.

Somali-Owned Businesses

Somali people possess traditional business insight. Many novice entrepreneurs with optimistic spirits hold the perception that their new businesses will bloom once they open their stores, and they will become rich. Such perception is pervasive, and it may contribute to the sudden upsurge of ambitious Somali businesspeople who are enthusiastically working long hours.

Today, Somali-owned businesses continue to be the foundation of employment in minority communities. Most Somali novice business owners in Saint Cloud did not do any research to determine whether their ideas had the potential to succeed.

Hormud Meat-Grocery Market Inc. at 3360 Division Street.

Somali American entrepreneurs often set up businesses in underserved retail markets and in neighborhoods where non-Somalis are reluctant to invest. They also open businesses in areas where there is a heavy concentration of Somalis.

As of spring 2017, Somalis own five restaurants, three coffee shops, and seven grocery stores in Saint Cloud. Most of those businesses cater solely to Somalis.

Types of Businesses

Somali business owners own a variety of enterprises. These include the aforementioned restaurants and grocery stores that sell ethnic food and other products, as well as clothing stores, money transfer agencies, tax return bureaus, insurance companies, taxi or truck transportation services, cell phone and computer repair shops, tailoring services, and barber shops. These Somali-owned businesses, no matter how big or small, offer services for their community's needs.

Somali entrepreneurs fulfill transportation needs in Saint Cloud and its environs through medical transport services. Tohow Siyad owns thirty-two medical transportation trucks. He started his business, National Home Health Care Transportation, in 2009, hiring a diverse mix of employees, including longtime residents, Indians, Somalis, and Sudanese.

Why Do Somalis Open
New Businesses?

Eight in ten Somali entrepreneurs who held college degrees said they started their own businesses because they could not get a good job that corresponded to their education level. Many college graduates fail to find suitable jobs, but they choose to be independent. Therefore, financial independence is probably the primary reason people open family-owned businesses.

Some other graduates feel their current part-time jobs do not help them pay the monthly bills well. Abdi Daisane, who graduated from St. Cloud State University in 2015, said, "Every one of us is going through a hard time when seeking a job. Some open their business. While the business is still in its early stages, some look for second job as a second income to their families." Abdullahi Gure graduated from St. Cloud State University in 2012 with a degree in sociology and criminal justice. Gure works as a licensed social worker at the Employment Action Center and is also the owner of a small business. Gure and his business partner Hamid Mahat, a lab technician, co-own the Iftin Grocery Store, which opened on December 15, 2015. Both partners indicated that they would expand their business soon so they could cater to all communities in the city. Gure is a hardworking young man who gets off his day job at 4:00 p.m. and then goes to the grocery until its 9:00 p.m. closing.

Many business owners felt that business formation rates were even higher among Somali Americans than other foreign-born nationalities or ethnicities.

What and to Whom They Cater

Somali business owners provide customers with hijabs and halal meat (meat from animals that have been slaughtered in the prescribed way according to the Sharia). According to Tohow, "Somali businesses cater not only to Somalis but also other foreign-born communities, such as fellow Africans, Asians, and Arabs." Tohow believes that Somali businesses are here in Saint Cloud to introduce other people to their culture and to help Somali Americans retain their culinary traditions and their way of dressing. He observes that Sudanese, Oromo, and Ethiopian nationals buy their ethnic foods and essential oils from Somali-owned grocery stores in the city.

Asha Elmi, a thirty-year-old Somali widow with five children, walks to nearby Pantown Plaza, a Somali mall on 3407 Third Street N., to pay her monthly house rent and car insurance, electric, Internet service provider, and cell phone bills. "Because of the growing number of Somali-owned businesses in this area, I don't have to struggle speaking in English to contact customer service. All my needs are catered under one roof, without the need to drive to different locations to pay bills," Asha said. Many recently arrived Somalis who have a language barrier like Asha's patronize Somali businesses because they offer quick, safe, and convenient payment systems.

Many Somalis, particularly the elderly, purchase money orders from Somali-owned stores. According to Abdirahim Osman, owner of Green Repairs and Services, "Because of language difficulties, recent immigrants have a hard time paying bills on the phone or online. To close that gap, our center helps those customers."

St. Cloud Karamel has small individual Somali-owned businesses.

In Saint Cloud, Somali entrepreneurs cater almost exclusively to Somalis in the area and its immediate surroundings. Owing to the availability of ethnic food, halal meat, and traditional herbs, most Somalis prefer to shop at Somali grocery stores.

Halima Muse, a mother of five kids, told me she's never bought anything from stores owned by non-Somalis like Coborn's and Lunds & Byerlys. When I asked her why not, she smiled at me and asked, "Would you get camel's meat, camel's milk, ghee, black seed, and fenugreek exported from Somalia from these stores?" Before I answered her question, she held my hand and looked at me in the eye and said, "Haven't you seen how Somali-owned malls buzz with boundless activity as customers buy food, groceries, clothes, and other items that can't be found at other stores in central Minnesota?" Halima's questions pushed me to focus on the relationship between Somali business owners and their Somali customers.

Somali businesses are budget friendly. For example, one of the managers of the Mogadishu Grocery said, "In case our customers run low on money while they're shopping, they grab anything they want from the stores and pay at the end of the month without any interest accrued."

Somali business owners assist families who are struggling financially due to the Somali cultural practice of supporting the community's needs. Even though business owners receive loans from their relatives when they are cash-strapped, assisting poor members of the community in the area is important. Somalis live in a tight-knit society that assists one another. Traditionally, the success of a Somali business depends upon the support of Somalis in the area.

The Somali-owned money remittance agencies also cater to Somalis and other immigrants in Saint Cloud and its environs. Today, Saint Cloud has ten Somali-owned money transfer agencies, known as *Hawala*. This is an Arabic word meaning *transfer*. The most popular money transfer agencies in Saint Cloud are Amal, Kaah Express, Dahabshil, Juba Express, and Mustaqbal. Today, Hawala has become a means of supporting Somali families back home in Somalia. According to Mohammed Yusuf, the director of the Kaah Express remittance agency, who opened two branches in Saint Cloud, "Most of my customers include Somalis and non-Somalis who wire their money back home. Among those customers are other East Africans, West Africans, Pakistanis, and Indians." Mohamud opened his first branch office inside of the Mogadishu Grocery.

Safiya Abdi, who works at a meat-processing plant, sends $400 to $600 back to her ailing parents and unemployed siblings in Somalia each month through money transfer agencies. "We would not have sent money to our families back home if we didn't have money transfer agencies in the Saint Cloud area." Why can't Somalis use other wiring companies like Western Union? A money transfer employee who declined to have his name mentioned in this book said that Western Union has not established bureaus in Somalia or neighboring refugee camps in Kenya and Ethiopia.

Regardless of how Somali business owners assist their community in Saint Cloud, there are several hurdles they face while navigating the American business system.

Barriers to Somali-Owned Business

Obviously, Somali business boosts Saint Cloud's economic growth, levels of employment, and community development. Yet small-business owners face immense obstacles that may hamstring their businesses. Those challenges include language and cultural barriers, along with a lack of credit history, access to capital, investment partnerships, access to business networks, legal counsel, business technical assistance, and accounting services.

Language and Cultural Barriers

One of the most conspicuous challenges to business is the language barrier—some entrepreneurs have a hard time understanding English. This may hinder or limit Somali entrepreneurs' access to business development resources, and expanding their clientele beyond the Somali community is important for profitability.

"For many in the Somali business community, it is often hard to learn how America's intricate business system works," said Tohow. "When one has limited English, understanding the business structure is far more challenging."[1]

Even though learning perfect English can open the doors to economic opportunity, some Somali business owners argue that they do not have the ambition to serve customers outside the Somali community. Because of this mind-set and the exclusively Somali clientele, novice entrepreneurs rely much on the use of their native Somali language when conducting their business.

Although they do not have a language barrier, younger entrepreneurs with advanced degrees are unfamiliar with systems that would help them broaden their fledgling businesses beyond the Somali community. Many of the graduates who run their own businesses work in a similar fashion to those who have limited language skills. Regardless of their educational status and language proficiency, their prime target is their own community using their native Somali business system. They lack the understanding of the US business system, including networking, mentoring, and finding financial resources. To bridge the knowledge gap, it is important for young entrepreneurs to be equipped with training on American business knowledge.

Poor Prior Research and Planning

Unfortunately, most Somali small-business owners open their businesses without plans and forethought. The belief that their new business will prosper is common among aspirants. "Many trust their own instincts," said Tarabi Jama, founder and executive director of Gateway, a business consulting firm. "Opening a business requires a clear understanding of the market that the new business owners are about to enter, how they are going to do it, and the people they are going to serve. Sadly, many new entrepreneurs do not explore their target market and write down their SWOT analysis to measure their strengths, weaknesses, opportunities, and threats." It is possible that most Somali entrepreneurs do not ask themselves who their ideal customers are, the number of competitors already in the market, why they are starting their new businesses, how the products or services they're offering will be different from those in the market before them, and the legal requirements.

"Most Somali businesses lack business strategies, vision, resources, and goals," said Tohow Siyad, who owns several businesses in Saint Cloud. "For example, when they are starting up a new business, they do not conduct any earlier research; neither do they know sources of investment that could help them start up."[2]

According to Mohamed Beene-Beene, executive director of the Minnesota Somali Chamber of Commerce, "Most new business owners do not strategize or seek advice about location and zoning laws. For instance, most of their businesses are not customer-friendly locations. Some do not comprehend the American business system."[3] When prospective businesspeople collect cash from their immediate families, relatives, and friends, they do not think they need financial coaching, business training, mentorship, and credit counseling. Many novice business owners make costly mistakes by not exploring markets adequately before they commit funds to their plans. According to Tarabi Jama:

> New business owners often jump to the execution of their business before they plan in advance. For example, when someone is going to do some restaurant business, he or she needs to make sure whether or not the business premises can be remodeled. It is also important for new business owners to license and learn information regarding

zoning issues before they rent any space for their business.[4]

According to some interviewees, one of the perceived obstacles Somali business owners often face is finding locations suitable for business growth. Farah Guled, manager of the Mogadishu restaurant, said, "The city hesitates to give us good strategic locations in which we can open up our businesses. Some wrong stereotypes that Somalis are loud and dirty could be the case, I think. Because of being cash-strapped, most Somali business owners do not have the economic capacity to own the business premises."[5] Tarabi argued:

> Many business owners open up their businesses in locations adjacent to their ethnic communities. Choosing a good location plays a pivotal role in the success and business diversification. Business owners have two advantages, reasonable monthly rent and proximity of their particular clients, but they miss the opportunity to attract non-Somali clients. The expandability of the market borderline largely depends on provisions for all consumers irrespective of a specific race or ethnicity.[6]

Another perceived obstacle facing the Somali business community is lack of capital to buy big business centers. Somali-owned retail stores, located within one building, are small. Farah stated, "One person cannot afford to rent a whole building by him or herself, particularly those novice entrepreneurs in Saint Cloud. We seek partners who are willing to pool our resources together so we can rent a spacious building."[7] Hared Jibril, owner of Hormud Meat & Grocery Market at 3360 W. Division Street, believes Somalis do not have the economic power to rent an entire building for themselves. Some other business owners disagreed with Jibril's idea and said they could receive any amount of money from their family members, immediate relatives, and friends, but they have a hard time understanding how American business systems work.

One of the perceived obstacles Somali businesspeople often cite is not being allowed to modify their rented buildings. Farah also mentioned facing challenges when remodeling their business premises. "When renting, property owners refuse us remodeling their buildings," said Farah. "On top of that, most of our malls were initially built to be offices, not for a particular business purpose. Because of that insurmountable hurdle, we cannot custom-build the buildings because of licensing agreements that hamper us." Tarabi talked about another possible problem, partnership disputes:

> When opening up a new business, Somalis often look for someone they know well to partner with. The two people pool their resources together and put up a new business without signing a written partnership agreement before an attorney. Disputes can arise from businesses that are solely formed on mutual trust because they do not have a written agreement in place.[8]

Even though Somali business partners do not have business disputes very often, a written partnership agreement is highly recommended. During my interviews, I learned that most business partners who hail from the same clan share a deep trust with each other. Therefore, the possibility of a business row in the Somali community is minimal. In case a dispute arises, a panel of local community elders and religious leaders may probe into the issues that pertain to the dispute. The elders who hold the mediation help the partners come to an agreement. To avoid confusion, Tarabi recommends prospective business partners put a well-drafted partnership contract in place to act as a guidepost.

Mogadishu Meat & Grocery Store at 1725 Seventh Street South, Saint Cloud, MN. This restaurant opened in 2008.

Lack of Access to Funding for Growth

Each business needs some type of investment and assistance so that it will have the ability to flourish and improve its products' quality and services. Business expansion and prospective financial crisis recovery hinge on receiving extra cash injections.

Many of the Somalis I interviewed said non-Somali entrepreneurs receive lines of credit and single-purpose loans from state and local governments for their small business growth, but Somalis find it difficult to obtain outside financing from non-Somali businesspeople or government agencies. This is because some new business owners may have poor, or no, past credit history. Most the Somali residents in Saint Cloud are renters, not homeowners. Most are new to the city and do not have enough wealth; equity in a home is a type of wealth lenders evaluate. Many of the business owners I've interviewed and spoken with in casual conversation said they left their property behind when they fled from Somalia. Therefore, most community members do not know people with good credit history who may have had financial vehicles in the past. Despite the challenges in obtaining capital to start or expand their businesses, entre-preneurs work with whatever money they have.

Mohammed Yusuf, the owner of Kaah Express, said that credit agencies put a lot of conditions on Somali-owned and managed businesses. "They want Somali entrepreneurs who have already taken loans and paid them back in time," Mohammed said. "Most lenders and banking institutions are very reluctant to offer us long-term loans to shore up our business. They, instead, ask us to show them whether we own fixed assets, land, and property so we would use such properties as collateral to secure the debt. Sadly, most of us never took loans in the past. Some never even owned a house or a car through a down payment. This creates a huge burden for a new business start-up."[9] This is true for everyone in the United States who is seeking a loan, but it is especially challenging for recent refugees and immigrants.

A few Somali business owners, particularly young entrepreneurs, are open to receiving loans, but they do not have the business expertise that can connect them with the proper financial institutions. "If we connect with mentors who are willing to assist us, we can seek outside financial assistance," said Zubeir, the twenty-four-year-old owner of Zubeir Tax and Insurance Agency.

Business owners echoed the claim that the city and business organizations are not assisting small-scale Somali entrepreneurs effectively. One business owner said, "Investors may prefer investing in larger companies owned by longtime resident owners because they assume we, Somalis, own small businesses that do not provide employment for the communities in central Minnesota."

Religion Restricts Loan Taking

For Somalis, religion and culture are closely linked. Both present a set of impediments to Somali entrepreneurs seeking outside financial assistance because Islam places restrictions on taking out loans with interest. As the Quran and Sharia law forbid usury, known in Arabic as *Riba*, Somali entrepreneurs avoid taking out loans with interest from banks, credit unions, or other credit agencies. Tohow explained how Somali business owners find their loans:

In case of financial difficulties, the business owners seek extra capital from their family members
or friends to support them. Seeking any financial
backing from their community members may not
involve the payment of interest rates and due dates.
The notion of "Pay me back when you can" encourages Somalis to seek financial assistance from their
immediate affluent relatives. When Somali business owners seek loans from their relatives, they do
not have to pay interest, and they can pay back the
money as it suits them. On the top of that, family
members or friends do not ask business aspirants
to show them whether or not they have prepared a
business plan. They ask them the loan they need to
start the business with, and then their family members or friends give them the loan right away.[10]

Even though seven of the ten Somali business owners I
interviewed reported that they were opposed to borrow-
ing money from banking and loan institutions as a source
of start-up capital, they said they might be interested in
seeking only Sharia-compliant finance if it were available
to them in their city. Only one young business owner was
interested in obtaining alternative loans or financial backing from the local banking institutions. However, a small

fraction of business owners said they were not interested in seeking assistance from either the conventional banking system or Islamic-based Riba-free institutions. This group argues that the Islamic banks often charge exorbitantly more than the conventional banking system.

Pantown Plaza has many individual stores.

Selling the Same Stuff

In recent times, several Somalis have opened identical competing businesses in Saint Cloud, creating an intense, adversarial atmosphere. When you visit the Somali-owned business malls, you can see clothing stores that sell the same clothes. For example, in five boutiques in the Mogadishu Mall, each stall sells the same women's beauty products, women's clothes, and jewelry. Tarabi Jama, the executive director of Gateway who gave thirty Somali business owners an eight-week long business course at the Saint Cloud Library, explained market saturation:

> The reason why Somali business owners sell the same garb can be attributed to many factors. One of the biggest factors includes poor market analysis. If the new business owners do not evaluate the market niche and understand the advantages and pitfalls of their new venture, they may not offer something more innovative than their competitors to attract customers. Today, more entrepreneurs target the same customer base and offer identical products and services.[11]

Some business owners told me they targeted the same customer base because they sold items with which they were familiar. A substantial majority of Somali business owners report that they often target their loyal customers, who are their own clan members, willing to buy whatever is carried in the stores. This means they do not target non-Somalis in the city as potential customers.

Tired of buying familiar products, large numbers of Somali people living in Saint Cloud often travel down to the Twin Cities to buy the latest fashions. During my interviews, I found that market saturation forced Somali business owners to sell their items cheaply. The combined market saturation and lack of willing customers may create challenges and a considerable profit loss. If Somali business owners do not integrate with other communities in the city, they will face more isolation and lack of expansion.

Lack of Business Networking, Mentoring, and Connections

Somali culture lacks three important components that expand businesses: networking, mentoring, and social connecting. Most Somalis who currently own businesses in the area are not aware of what business networking means. During networking, people increase their knowledge, obtain new clients, and share their business information with others. In America, business networking is highly encouraged. However, in the Somali culture, this is virtually nonexistent. Somali business owners do not meet to expand their businesses' profitability. They share information by word of mouth, and men and women socialize differently. Most male Somali business owners said that they gather in the restaurants, grocery stores, coffee shops, and mosques to share community information. Such meetings are informal, unorganized, and will not have anything specifically to do with business expansion. Unlike men, women entrepreneurs barely socialize for business reasons. They stay home to look after their families after their business hours.

Another element that hampers business is the absence of connection. Most Somali business owners do not value connections with other ethnicities and communities in the city. If you invite a new Somali business owner to join local business agencies, they bluntly question why you want to include them. Most are not familiar with the importance of business associations, such as the Saint Cloud Area Chamber of Commerce and other local business entities. "We don't have any Somali-owned businesses as members right now," said Teresa Reed Bohnen, president of the Saint Cloud Area Chamber of Commerce. "We have been working with their employers in the Diversity Council to work closely with many more minority-owned businesses of all types joining the Chamber," she added.

Abdi Mahad, a research analyst, contended that:

Because of their different business customs, Somalis do not prioritize becoming part of the Chamber of

Commerce unless they get trainings and business coaching from someone who looks like them. Once they are trained about American business methods, they will be able to become integrated into the greater social fabric of the community.[12]

When Somali business owners decide to change their habits and join, they will meet new people and widen their connections. Those connections will lead to finding new opportunities, skills, diverse markets, and business investment.

Mentoring, learning from other successful businesspeople, is another important element that Somali business owners lack. Mentoring often helps business owners increase performance, skills, professionalism, and profitability in their companies

Mentoring, social connecting, and business networking are important tools for business owners. Therefore, Somali entrepreneurs should be encouraged to build relationships and expand networks.

Women Business Owners

In the wake of the collapse of Somalia's central government in 1990, Somali women played an important role in economic and social development. During the conflict, the male-dominated jobs were terminated. The women stood up to salvage the country and the people. For many novice female entrepreneurs in Somalia, entering the world of business was a necessity to save their families. Even though women had little access to traditional business loans from their relatives, some had no other choice but to sell their property and golden jewelry to launch their ventures. To survive, women became their families' primary breadwinners.

Khadija Khalif's clothing and jewelry store at the new Safari Mall.

In Somalia, women did not face as many hurdles as they are facing today in Saint Cloud and the United States in general. There, small-business owners did not have to learn English or navigate through the complexity of the American business structure. The business start-up did not require a lot of paperwork and contracts. They rented a building and paid a monthly rent. Some did not need a physical business location. They sold food and various other products in an open bazaar. They also did not need a lot of planning and financial resources to get started. They were well aware of the traditional Somali business system. In addition to that, female entrepreneurs did not worry about childcare because they lived with their parents or grandparents who could look after the babies.

"As the Somali civil war intensified, women were targeted from all sides, forcing women business owners to sell their businesses and leave home," said Marian Yusuf, a business owner. "When women who left their husbands back home came to Saint Cloud with their children, they began working very hard in many shifts at local factories. They met culture, language, weather, and business systems very different from what they knew back home." When they came to Minnesota, they faced even greater difficulties due to their limited English skills. Some of those women began working long hours in meat-processing plants. Even working married couples found they couldn't cover household expenses because their combined salaries were meager. Because of the current climate of economic uncertainty and massive job losses due to the last recession, many husbands remain unemployed. Former female business owners are again standing up to play an active role in opening small-scale businesses to sustain their families. Today, Somali women own twenty-six registered businesses throughout Saint Cloud. Many of these include clothing stores and boutiques. Women are steadily increasing their numbers as small-business owners.

Not all female entrepreneurs are illiterate; some have degrees from Somali schools. One of the most significant obstacles hindering women's progress in small businesses is the cultural setting that complicates things for women who want to start and run enterprises. According to Shamhad, the owner of a women's clothing store on Thirty-Third Street, "Female business aspirants often have trouble raising capital to start up. Men are much more likely than women to secure their funding from business partners." Some women take loans from their family members, relatives, and friends to begin their own businesses. Some others become members of a community based financial rotation system known as in Somali as *Ayuuto* ("aiuto"), which means *assistance* in the Italian language. This is also known as microfinance. Everyone brings the same amount of money to place in a pool while one person may take the money pool every month.

Mini Somali women's clothing stores at Saint Cloud Karamel LLC.

Because women do not get the necessary financial backing for their enterprises, they start small-scale businesses that do not involve big initial investments. According to Zeinab Mohamed, the owner of the Zeinab Clothing

Store at Mogadishu Meat & Grocery Store, "Traditionally, I did not open my store to create wealth. I started it to help my family and raise my children. I always want to enjoy independence and economic freedom. My ambition is to identify a customer-friendly location and seek business expansion, so that my children will inherit from me in the future."[13]

Today, women own an array of microbusinesses that often face low growth and low profits. Many business owners are also facing reduced demand for their products and services. Shamhad said, "Women often start their businesses with fewer resources available to them than men. The lack of attainability of good capital and poor accessibility of familial investment drive women to focus on small-scale retail stores that merely sell Somali women's clothing because they can't afford to open a big business like male business counterparts do. For example, Somali business owners run businesses like money transfer agencies, grocery stores, insurance agencies, and restaurants. Their main customers are women; however, women are not the owners of those businesses."[14]

Zeinab states that women can collect capital and rent business premises on their own, but the challenge is most women are blithely unaware of how to navigate the American business system, legal aspects of renting a business location, and other regulations that would expand their businesses.

Another barrier for women, unlike their male counterparts, is they must split their time between maintaining the traditional family and running the business. They have less time to spend than do men on their companies. Because of multitasking, some women-owned clothing stores open around noon after the owners cook their family meals. "I often have trouble balancing between my family life and my work," said Shamhad. "I drop off and pick up my kids from school in the afternoon." Most of those female entrepreneurs left their spouses back home in Somalia. In the United States, they play a dual role in parenting in an environment and culture challenging to them and their work.

Conclusion

Many women business owners, unlike men, are open to gaining access to financial assistance and are ready to overcome obstacles to expand their small-scale businesses. Women can take advantage of specific programs that are tailored to their needs. Many women business owners echo the opinion that women are more likely than their male counterparts to engage in programs that will teach them techniques to advance their businesses.

Before women start businesses, they should have a robust social network, sound capital, guidance, mentorship, and an altruistic support system in place. When women take advantage of a support network of people willing to help them step by step, the chance for business growth is immense.

Recommendation

For Somali business owners to modernize and expand their business and clientele, integration is required. Businesspeople should reach out to those who are active and capable of connecting them to the local business community, through the Chamber of Commerce, Business and Professional Women's Foundation, and Business Network International. To encourage more participation, the Chamber should consider waiving or reducing membership fees. For increased profits, Somali business owners should have Somali and non-Somali customers.

Chapter 6

NEW IMMIGRANTS' HEALTH CHALLENGES

Whatever you hide, hides you.

—Somali proverb

EVERY TIME I HELP A FAMILY MEMBER in the emergency room at the St. Cloud Hospital, I see dozens of Somalis in the waiting area. After having conversations with some of the patients, I've concluded that they visit the emergency room for various reasons: (1) no experience with the idea and practice of preventative medicine; (2) no trust of medications that might violate Islamic religious precepts; (3) inability to follow through with scheduled clinic appointments; (4) cultural practices; (5) affordability of care; and (6) reluctance to recognize and address the topic of mental illness. To get to know why most of the recently arrived Somalis rely solely on the hospital, it is crucial to delve into the existing challenges keeping them from receiving proper care from their primary physicians.

When health-care professionals and their consumers do not share the same language, culture, ethnicity, and socioeconomic and educational background, health-care professionals face many obvious difficulties that slow the delivery of quality health care for Somali patients.

Cultural Beliefs

Somalis brought their customs, rituals, and health-care beliefs and practices with them. Despite a growing Somali population in Saint Cloud, American health providers are still grappling to understand the Somali cultural approach to health care. Delivering broad health care to Somali patients means understanding their beliefs and practices. In the United States, Somalis have had to learn about certain diseases and ailments that they were not familiar with back home. Most people are already familiar with malaria, cholera, jaundice, tuberculosis, and measles.

Definition of *Health* and *Illness*

Health is "the condition of being well or free from physical or psychological disease and illness."[1] *Illness* is a specific condition that prevents one's body or mind from working normally or at optimum capability. American health-care professionals and their Somali patients do not define the two terms—*health* and *illness*—in the same way. To understand the Somali view of health and illness, it is crucial to look at Somalis' culture and religious practices. Somalis almost universally can be categorized by their staunch adherence to Islam, which shapes all aspects of Somali culture, including their approach to wellness.

*Ismael Khalif, the owner of Afya Pharmacy
on 3407 Third St. North, Saint Cloud.*

When new Somalis arrive in the United States, they find health care very different from that back home in Somalia. Some of the greatest hurdles the new immigrants face include their inadequate health literacy, religious practices, cultural barriers, and limited English skills, which are impediments to following good health-care practices here.

No Tradition of Preventative Medicine

Somalis do not seek out preventative care because they only go to the doctor when they are sick. Health professionals do all they can to try to prevent health problems, but it is hard to change the Somali people's mind-set, to encourage them to go to the doctor when healthy. In Africa, Somali patients go to their doctor after they have tried faith healing and herbal remedies. Thus, a medical doctor is a last resort. One reason could be that Somalis used herbs for a long time before they were exposed to Western medications.

Medication Suspicion

It is common for Somalis to question their doctors about whether recommended medication contains gelatin because Islam teaches that medicines laced with pork or alcohol are to be avoided. "Oftentimes, some late-arriving refugees confuse gluten with gelatin," said Ismael Khalif. "Understanding prescription information is essential for the Somali community in the Saint Cloud area."[2] During my interviews, I found that the English language barrier could be one of the main reasons Somalis are suspicious of taking Western medication. A non-Somali nurse said, "The older people who have never had postsecondary education may appear to avoid taking Western medicine while the younger generation does not experience any problem at all."

Some nurses told me that Somali patients often have large numbers of visitors. Visiting the sick to pray for a cure is an important part of a Muslim's duties. In Islam, it is obligatory for families and friends to visit their hospitalized loved ones. It is common to see community members unrelated to the ailing patient come to visit the hospital wards. Hospital visitation purposes may vary. Some close families help the admitted patient with interpretation and some others bring traditional Somali food because patients are suspicious of pork products added to the hospital meals. In some cases, accredited religious scholars and mosque imams offer a special prayer for those hospitalized patients. At hospital wards, clergy provide the patients with emotional and faith-healing support.

Understanding Religious and Cultural Practices

Somali people are staunch Sunni Muslims. Most rely upon medieval medical practices that are deeply entrenched in the Islamic religion and prophetic traditions. As usual, Somali people's health practices, including prevention and treatment of certain ailments and symptoms, are significantly affected by numerous variables including culture, religious beliefs, and linguistic considerations.

Many Somalis believe that an individual cannot prevent illness. The notion that God brings both health and sickness is prevalent among Somalis. Most of the people I spoke with said God created human beings for a test; illness is part of it, a test of how strongly a person believes in God. Most entertain the idea that human beings were brought to this world to suffer, which is why many Somalis feel they are predestined to get good and bad health before they are even born; if one is sick, it is fate and there is nothing one can do about it. The best way to prevent themselves from the ailments is to adhere to the five pillars of Islam, recite the Quran, and practice prayer. One old Somali patient once told me, "God is the divine physician and the healer of our souls and bodies. We can turn to him when we are sick and we seek his healing." Most Somalis believe healing occurs when one draws closer to God and experiences moral and spiritual change.

If a doctor's appointment coincides with one of the main festivals in the Islamic calendar, such as Eid al-Fitr and Eid al-Adha, it's highly likely the patient will skip the visit. Besides Muslim holidays, most Somalis avoid appointments during the month of Ramadan if drawing blood is involved. Somali patients are also more likely to skip an appointment scheduled on a Friday between 11:00 a.m. and 1:00 p.m., because Friday is a significant day for Muslims and a special congregational prayer known as a *Salatul Jumu'ah* is performed at noon. The Friday prayer is an obligation upon every capable Muslim.

A non-Somali nurse that I interviewed told me she sensed how Somali patients' strict adherence to their faith and culture shapes their view of Western medicine:

One day I gave medicine to a Somali man, and he read a few verses of Quran over the medicine before he swallowed it. When I asked him what he was doing, he said through the interpreter that the Quran would help the medicine work better. Also, sometimes Somali patients refuse treatment due to their fasting.[3]

Cultural Practices Differ from Prevailing American Culture

Because of differences concerning health practices, a deep chasm is widening between Somalis and non-Somali medical practitioners. Many of my interviewees echoed that Somalis' distinctive learned cultural behaviors and beliefs play an important role in refugee people's health. A Somali man recounted his experiences in some hospitals. He explained:

> Every time I step in a hospital, I see too many prying eyes looking at me. I ask myself, do I look like someone who fell off another planet? Do they think I am carrying plenty of transmittable diseases? Sadly, some nurses and doctors do not have the knowledge and competencies to work with immigrant and refugee patients. Even if the hospitals have interpreters, perceptions towards recent arriving refugees will never change until the hospital staff are educated and trained in ways to deliver culturally responsive care. What most doctors do not know, as far as I know, is the importance of showing open-mindedness and sympathy to their patients who don't look like them. In order for clients to trust doctors, the clinics must be a

welcoming and safe environment. The hospital staff must demonstrate compassion and cultivate a trusting relationship with their patients. They also must learn how our own cultural values, beliefs, and assumptions influence their delivery of care. I advise to some hospital staff to learn strategies that prevent negative attitudes and stereotyping in health services.

I also see many Somali patients who view their doctors wrongly. My advice for them is we have come to a new country with a different medical system; we need to do what people before us do when it comes to prevention, immunization, and taking required dosages. You can't be your own doctor. You can't take one's medicine assuming you two share a similar ailment. We don't have to rely on some herbal medicine, voodoo, and charlatans. We need to trust our own doctors.[4]

Doctor Preference

Modesty is extremely important for Muslims. Most Somali patients, particularly women, are reluctant to expose their bodies to a nurse or a doctor. It is critical that health-care providers prevent any unnecessary exposure.

A few female Somalis said they would prefer to see a female nurse and doctor. Some women clearly stated they have a right to refuse a male doctor or male interpreter. Eight out of ten Somali women I interviewed about the issue said they felt uncomfortable talking to male doctors and nurses about health-related issues. They also agreed that they were uncomfortable talking to a female doctor and nurse in the presence of a male interpreter.

Although women are given a choice of health-care professionals for their medical care, not all Somali women choose a female doctor. I am a woman, and I have a male doctor. I regard and interact with him as a doctor, not simply as a man.

Contraception and Cesarean Section

Most Somali women who are opposed to pap smears / swab testing prefer urine testing. However, many women I spoke with indicated they would cancel appointments if either test were involved. Birth control is not widely practiced because Somalis prefer large families. Some traditional couples believe that contraceptive methods interfere with God's will. But some women have no problems with using contraception to space their children and will, therefore, work with a medical professional.

Valuing family is a distinctive aspect of the Somali culture, so parents and extended family make important decisions for their loved ones about hospital admissions, the administration of certain drugs, and surgical procedures. For example, during a woman's childbirth, her husband often is involved in the decision-making process regarding an operation. Most husbands convince their wives not to undergo a Cesarean section because they believe it will hinder their abilities to conceive and give birth to further children. Another impediment to a woman's free choice is the major role the mother-in-law plays in decisions regarding surgery. A nurse informed me that a woman in delivery who was writhing in pain refused to take painkillers or an epidural in the presence of her in-laws. Once the in-laws stepped outside of the room, she requested the painkillers. Oftentimes, the man's family members presume allowing medicine to a woman in labor will cause a stillbirth or some type of birth defect. A few young married women confided to me that their in-laws controlled their decision-making power regarding their health-care needs.

Most Somali women in the United States argue that Western doctors rush to perform a Cesarean section. Traditionally, women in Africa are in labor for many days. The vast majority of women give birth vaginally. In the past, Cesarean sections were not part of the Somali culture. Today, most hospitals in Somalia perform C-sections, but the number of surgeries is not as high as in the United States. Many women ask for the procedure of their own accord. "I have seven children," Halima Adan said. "Three children were born in Kenya without surgery, while I delivered four children by C-section in the US. Now I can say if a mother has a C-section once, she'll need another if she gets pregnant again. I am afraid that the risks of surgery will go up with each procedure." Halima claims that natural births are decreasing in the West considerably because the procedure is easy and lucrative.

Abortion is only permitted when the mother's life is in real danger. The Quran commands Muslims not to kill their children for fear that they can't provide them with sustenance. The Somali Islamic scholars I have spoken to said that Islam recognizes the fetus in a mother's womb as a human life.

Diabetes

It's important to understand the prevalence of diabetes among Somalis in the area. According to CentraCare's estimates, more than 11,700 patients who identify themselves as Somali suffer diabetes.[5]

Diabetes does not only affect adults but also Somali children in Minnesota, who suffer from type 1 diabetes at higher rates than non-Somalis do.[6]

Six in ten Somali seniors told me they had diabetes. Sadly, most have no clue about what type they have. I also found that most rely upon traditional Somali medications to lower their high risk of complications. A few patients alternate insulin with ethnic herbs once they have been diagnosed.

Some patients in my family told me they never had diabetes until they came to the United States. "In Africa, we walked miles and miles all of the time to get to and from work. In the US, we rely upon cars too much. That's why many of us have so many health complications," said one of community elders, who has diabetes.

Traditionally, Somalis consume pasta, rice, bread, meat, sugary tea, and many other fast foods made with white flour. A few interviewees maintained a sedentary life-style, consumed excessive sugar, and followed an unhealthy diet, a lifestyle that has clearly contributed to the increase in diabetes.

When a patient is diagnosed with diabetes, his or her family members make the decision as to whether the patient requires a second opinion or should take the medicine prescribed. Some seek other doctors or ask for further examination. Many believe diabetes affects only obese individuals. "Diabetes can occur at any age," said a nurse from CentraCare who prefers to remain anonymous. "It also affects those who are not overweight." To improve diabetes care and outcomes for East African populations in Stearns County, CentraCare holds many awareness programs tailored to enhance patient satisfaction and experience, reduce disparities in care, and make more community resources available.[7]

During my interviews, I found that Somali women were less likely than their male counterparts to go to a fitness center. A close female relative who suffers from diabetes explained to me why this is. "Somali women have little time for fitness activities since they do all household work and bear the primary responsibility of caring for their children. Women are hesitant to wear tight-fitting clothing, particularly when in the presence of males. Therefore, it is important to make available a gender-exclusive fitness program for Somali immigrant women." The city actually has a women-only public fitness facility known as Curves, but most Somali women do not know this.

The local hospital and surrounding clinics should teach the Somali community the importance of a healthy diet and regular physical activity through outreach from professional fitness trainers, dietitians, and Somali community health workers. Local doctors should disseminate culturally relevant educational materials about diabetes written in Somali.

Dental Health

Another problem in the Somali community is poor dental health. The number of dental issues we see is staggering. In Africa, because Somalis ate fresh foods all the time, cavities were not an issue. Because of the change in diet to processed foods in the United States, the Somali people get many cavities very quickly. Cavities usually cause them pain, so they need medicine. Many Somalis tell me they do not go to a dentist for cleaning or routine dental checkups. They resort to seeing their dentist only when they want to have their teeth extracted. Also, they are not used to dental flossing.

"Somali oral health practices have changed upon their arrival to the US," said one nurse. "Many gave up using a natural tooth-cleaning stick—commonly referred to in Somali as an *aday*, or in Arabic as a *miswak*—because they are not widely used in the United States. It's common to see Somalis attributing their cavities to lack of properly using chewing sticks for dental hygiene." Many other interviewees said they had dental problems a few months after their arrival from Somalia due to lack of proper insurance. Those who lack coverage are far less likely to visit their dentist for regular preventive checkups and treatment of cavities. Those Somali Americans travel outside of the United States for dental implants or bridges.

Traditional Medicine

My non-Somali friends have asked me about the smell of Somali people's bodies and clothes. Traditionally, Somalis apply ethnic essential oils for both relaxation and treatment of muscle aches, blemishes, burns, dry skin, and minor skin rashes; they also add plenty of spices to their foods, and these are emitted through the body. I am afraid some friends may interpret this odor as unhygienic, which is not the case.

Somalis, mostly elders, apply traditional oils made from black seeds, aloe vera, fenugreek, sesame, myrrh, frankincense, and many herbs native to Somali territory. Various older family members who rely upon herbs told me that this traditional Somali medicine helps them improve digestion and metabolism, boost immunity, and maintain overall health. For instance, black seed oils are used to treat diabetes, high cholesterol, hypertension, asthma, body aches, swelling, and many other maladies. This type of oil is also known as "the seed of blessing." Some Islamic scholars told me the Prophet Mohammed called black seed oil "a remedy for all diseases except death."

Most male elders use fenugreek to treat back pain and erectile dysfunction and other male problems. A Somali herbalist who treats Somali seniors in central

Minnesota with his herbal concoction told me fenugreek helps lower cardiovascular ailments, type 1 and 2 diabetes, blood glucose, and cholesterol levels. Married women use some plant roots and tree barks to deodorize their bodies and home. Their private parts are to be perfumed with homemade incense known as *oud, attar,* and *uunsi*. Some of these scented resins and incense are used for religious rituals. Apart from using oils and plant roots to treat common illnesses, traditional medicine men do burning, cupping, and laceration of the body. Many Somalis bear the scars of fire burning or lacerations. Traditional healers burn the skin near the area affected by jaundice, hepatitis, or other diseases. An old Somali proverb says, *"Dab iyo xanuun meel ma wada galaan,"* which literally means, *Pain and burning can't go hand in hand;* if the patient is cauterized, his or her pain goes away immediately.

Affordability of Care

Even though health-care reform improved access to affordable, quality health insurance for most Americans, the Somali community still faces innumerable barriers as they navigate the health-care system. Somali residents say they face enormous challenges in finding health-care programs that are good for them and their families. Part of the problem is that immigrants and refugees often work in industries less likely to offer health insurance and comprehensive plans. Even though most Somalis work long hours at several low-paying jobs, they either do not receive health insurance or are unable to pay for the full cost of their care. Ironically, those who get insurance through their work don't know how to enroll in the insurance plans that are available to them. That is why most newly arrived Somalis experience unique hurdles in accessing better health services. Only a few Somalis are aware of the existing federal or state healthcare assistance programs that give help to low-income children, pregnant women, and people living with disabilities.

"Before the refugees arrive in the US, medical practitioners at the refugee camps in Africa make sure that none of those refugees who are allowed resettlement in the US carry any transmittable diseases," said Abdi Mahad. "When the Somali refugees are resettled, they are eligible for temporary health insurance, but they have only eight months to seek free health care." During these months, caseworkers can link the newly arrived refugees with primary healthcare services who can assess their health and follow up on conditions identified overseas.

"Once new refugees arrive here, our agency gives a cultural orientation, and we encourage them to undergo regular checkups within that period," said Fathiya Mohamed, refugee program supervisor at Lutheran Social Services. "We set up refugee health screening appointments with clinics in the city once they arrive."[8]

Another big barrier to proper health care is that patients' names are often misspelled on their insurance cards, and then, they are denied coverage because "it isn't technically them." Most medical facilities reject a claim if the name on the insurance card does not match the patient's name. Patients should confirm that their insurance information, including the spelling of their names, is up to date when visiting their doctors' offices.

Medicaid insurance, allocated for the new refugees, only pays for certain medical services, such as visits to the doctor, prescription drugs, and hospitalization. Once those eight months expire, federal medical assistance can no longer cover their hospital visits and medical bills. The recent refugees are expected to pay for their individual health-care packages. A few hospitals offer financial aid that assists patients up to six months. When this coverage ends, most refugee patients stop seeing their doctors. First of all, the concept and acquisition of health-care insurance is literally foreign to many Somali refugees. Those working can't even afford a comprehensive health-care package. "Without regular access to affordable care," said Abdirizak, a patient care extender, "most Somali patients may suffer from preventable illness and injury. People need to be told about the importance of regular checkups and vaccination."[9]

During my conversations with Somali nurses, I found that Somali patients who have job-based insurance are most likely to use emergency room care once they get sick. "There is an overuse of emergency department services," said Abdirizak. "Many patients fail to follow up with their primary care physicians. Some of those patients are either oblivious to alternative care settings that can provide more effective treatment for their current ailments, or have some other linguistic impediments." Insured and uninsured patients I spoke to said language difficulty and a lack of reliable transportation were common barriers that kept them from meeting with a primary care physician.

Language and Cultural Barriers

Even though most hospitals and clinics provide free interpretation services, Somalis admit that seeking medical advice in a new country can be nerve-racking. They believe "everything" is different from their countries of origin. Doctors also think caring for foreign-born patients who speak little or no English can be an issue. Many of the Somalis I talked to stated that they had a hard time calling their doctor's office in advance to either reschedule or cancel their appointments. Instead of calling, they chose simply to skip them. "Hospitals often send their patients notification letters reminding them of their next appointments," said Ismael Khalif, the owner of Afya Pharmacy, Saint Cloud. "Limited English proficient refugees push their mail envelopes aside without understanding the contents they carry." After people visit their health-care facilities, they receive a survey in the mail asking them about their recent treatment. Patients with limited English language skills have a hard time telling their doctors their concerns, complaints, questions, or compliments about the care they've received. It is clear that patients' language difficulties and miscommunications often result in noncompliance with hospital/clinic follow-up, and misunderstanding prescription instructions and treatment. To bridge the gap between doctors and non-English speaking patients regarding medication use, Afya Pharmacy helps its clientele. The need to understand prescription information is critical to the community. In addition to this, the Walgreens on Division Street near Caribou Coffee also has a Somali-speaking pharmacist now.

The language barrier not only contributes to misdiagnosis and inaccurate prescriptions but also creates the misuse, overuse, and abuse of medications. More older adults are at high risk of prescription drug abuse because they often take more than one prescription each day. There's also an increased risk for mistakes regarding drug interactions. Prescription drug abuse is the fastest-growing problem within many Somali families.

"Old Somali patients may have a hard time understanding dosages. Some will stop the medications when the symptoms ease," Khalif said. Khalif often calls his customers when their prescription refill's near. "When they do not come here, I go to see them in person." Khalif does more than assist with his clients' needs. He helps them manage their medications and advises them to work with their health-care providers. He attributes customers' confusion to lack of knowledge and prior education. "In order for people to take their medications well, I drive up to their homes and sit with my consumers to explain to them about the importance of medication."

Interpretation

According to a US Census Bureau report examining the use of language in US hospitals and clinics, over 20 percent of Americans speak a language other than English at home. Of this population, more than 24 percent report they do not speak English well or do not speak English at all.[10]

I once witnessed a Somali grandfather going for a routine follow-up appointment, using his twelve-year-old granddaughter as a family interpreter. Deep down, I thought the young child might lack sufficient linguistic or conceptual abilities to facilitate doctor-patient communication. Everyone needs medical care at one point or another. Patients with limited English skills are entitled to have an interpreter, at no charge. The hospital and clinics in the Saint Cloud area use professional interpreters and sometimes friends or family members in an emergency. Patients have the right to the complete privacy and confidentiality of their personal medical information.

Some doctors I contacted said they've used informal interpreters as a short-term measure for emergency consultations. Most non-English speaking patients told me they relied on their children as ad hoc medical interpreters. Some of my relatives with limited English abilities told me they might prefer their children and grandchildren to interpret on their behalf, rather than a professional interpreter.

Ali Mohamud, who suffered a stroke in 2007, said:

I ask my son to accompany me to my medical appointments. I feel frustrated because most doctors do not want my son to help us interpret. Most non-Somali doctors do not know how we, Somalis, heavily rely on our own family members as our main interpretation and other medical support network. In my case, my son knows my health conditions well. I know the fact that he has not been trained and assessed in medical interpreting, but he grew up in the US. I am not saying he has mastered the medical terminology.[11]

Ali's son Ahmed, who goes to Tech High, said:

My father has difficulty in speaking and walking. Due to the problem of his slurred speech, he can't explain about his health. I know what he is going through well. I know whether or not he takes his medication and what dosage he takes. Many times in the past, doctors kicked me out and then they let me in for more information because my father couldn't speak for himself.[12]

Oftentimes, I see clinics or offices "forgetting to get an interpreter," and then they end up sending the client away. This is another huge barrier to proper health care because it is already difficult for this community to get transportation to their appointments. In addition to that, some patients skip work to see their doctors. If they get turned away, it is so hard for them to come back another day for an appointment. Zeinab Abdi complained about the problem of not seeing her doctor because of interpreter absence:

> In some situations, the front desk receptionists may feel that there is still a chance the interpreter will arrive. The hired interpreters must be reminded of their responsibility to show up. The hospitals do not have any idea how hard it is for me to set up another appointment. My daughter skips her class to give me a ride to and back from the clinic.[13]

Many patients show dissatisfaction with interpreters when discussing some medical conditions with their physicians. One patient informed me he was afraid of seeing a Somali interpreter in the room because he thought the interpreter might share his medical conditions with his close-knit community members. Instead of talking to his doctor about his pain, he chose to hide it. There are many taboo subjects that Somalis don't discuss in public. Most will avoid talking about sensitive subjects, such as rape, child abuse, domestic violence, mental illness, sexually transmitted diseases, cancer screening, and immunization in front of professional or ad hoc family interpreters.

Somali parents in central Minnesota told me their children acted as interpreters two to four times in the last six months. Yet some parents have reservations about allowing this. Halima, who refused to have her last name mentioned in the book, said that she was diametrically opposed to the idea of her children playing the role of informal interpreter. This view was supported by many other parents, who argued that their children are unsuitable to the task of interpreting health encounters.

Reluctance to Recognize and Address Mental Health

One of my interviewees, who declined to have her name mentioned here, came to the United States with her mom and her two grandparents. She told me her mom and her grandpa struggled with mental illness and went undiagnosed for nearly two decades. They didn't get the treatment they needed until their pain had affected her entire family. She experiences stress at home due to taking care of her ailing mother and grandparents for so long. She admitted to suffering from mood swings, acute bouts of anxiety, explosive tantrums, and panic attacks but is afraid to look for treatment for fear people will say she is crazy. "My mother dealt with severe depression after two militiamen killed my dad in front of us," said the woman. "The doctors said that Mom had schizophrenia while my grandpa battled the late stages of Parkinson's disease. None of our family had ever heard these two terms before we came to the US. Therefore, we refused to seek further professional counseling and medical intervention." Many Somali people experience mental health problems. Some interviewees told me that their close family members were experiencing depression and post-traumatic stress disorder and depended on their families for help; however, some families are unaware of the availability and accessibility to Western mental health services. I spoke with mental health professionals who stated that families' support is crucial for a patient's mental stability.

Because of the stigma surrounding psychiatric treatment and counseling, and not understanding mental health, Somali mental patients face cultural and community hurdles. So first, what is mental illness?

Definition

It is significant to note that there is no agreement about the definition of mental health between Somalis and Western mental health practitioners. Somali people do not have many terms to describe mental illnesses. Somali Americans commonly said mental illness starts when the symptoms affect the person's everyday life. For instance, when the patient starts randomly yelling, hitting others, or walking naked, then his family realizes he is insane. The words *crazy* or *insane*, known in Somali as *Waali*, are the only terms to describe individuals with psychiatric symptoms. Apart from these terms, there are words for stress (*welwel*), bipolar disorder (*Laba-miire*), and many others, but most Somalis do not connect these terms with mental illness.

According to Asad Mohamed, the founder and executive director of a Minnesota-based service dedicated to improving mental health treatment and services, "The term *mental illness* refers to a wide-ranging category of conditions, most of which do not involve lunacy, such as depression, anxiety disorders, eating disorders, attention deficit disorder (ADD), bipolar disorder, substance use, obsessive-compulsive disorder (OCD), and many more. Families of mental illness patients avoid talking about depression and anxiety disorders because they are afraid of being labeled as crazy."[14]

Even though mental illness represents a major health problem worldwide, the prevalence increases for Somalis after their arrival in the United States. Sadly, there are no official statistics on the number of Somali people who suffer from psychosocial disorders in central Minnesota. What we know for sure is most Somalis do not admit to having psychiatric problems; neither do they seek medical intervention and treatment.

After talking to some local mental health workers, I learned that several factors affect the current low care-seeking rates for Somalis in the Saint Cloud area. Patients and their families are not aware of the availability of mental health treatments; many fear stigma surrounding mental illness; and others prefer to use traditional medicine / faith healing.

To learn more about the scale of mental illness in the Somali community, I talked with Asad Mohamed, who opened Recover Health Resources (RHR) in Minneapolis, where he treats many patients. Asad is a forty-three-year-old Somali American who moved from Colorado to Minneapolis. He spent most of his career in computer science, but works these days to reduce the rate of mental illness within his Somali community. He explained why he chose to open his center:

I was assisting a close friend's adult day care. I witnessed too many Somali seniors who had unfounded fears. Some did not want to close the bathroom door. Sometimes when I closed the door, they yelled at me and told me they saw someone coming to harm them. They began acting out and screaming at other times and not following instructions. After having seen the prevalence of untreated mental health issues within the Somali community and the shortage of culturally appropriate mental health services in Minnesota, the idea of opening a center came to my mind. In 2014, I started Recover Health Resources (RHR) in Minneapolis and hired mental health professionals. I did not want to name the center [anything] like mental health institution, or mental health clinic. I knew Somali patients might choose not to associate themselves with mental health clinic to avoid psychiatric labels.[15]

Because of transportation issues, patients in central Minnesota had a hard time traveling to Minneapolis to seek culturally appropriate counseling, so Asad opened another branch in Saint Cloud in 2016. Asad stated:

Today Recover Health Resources in Minneapolis has five licensed professionals, one registered nurse, and twenty-three mental health practitioners while three professionals and six interns work at RHR in Saint Cloud. We have 172 clients in Minneapolis and 54 in Saint Cloud coming to the centers for mental evaluation and treatment.[16]

Mental health isn't isolated to one particular ethnic, cultural, or religious group; it affects everybody. Somali American nurses and health workers in Saint Cloud tell me many Somali seniors are also vulnerable to post-traumatic stress, depression, and other mental health problems. "Some are prone to numerous psychiatric symptoms and disorders due to their previous exposure to civil war and the loss of family members," said Farhiya Idifle, a social worker who graduated from St. Cloud State University in 2015 with a degree in social work. "These conditions, coupled with isolation, accelerate depression, particularly among women and older adults. Socioeconomic hardships and recurrent conditions of unemployment also trigger some forms of stress. The seniors were brought here while still heartbroken and desolate. They do not have friends with whom they can associate. Their kids often go for work or for fun while the seniors stay home and do nothing. Therefore, the impact of loneliness considerably affects the seniors. Above all, their lack of English skill isolates them further."[17]

Asad believes that mental illness in the Somali community is common because "protracted conflict, instability, and political persecution and torture, coupled with the widespread malnutrition or famine in Somalia, have had a large impact on the mental and psychological well-being of its people. Somali people in the US show some traumatic experiences in their lives. Some others have experienced adjustment challenges." While interviewing Somalis, I heard from many that difficult living conditions in their new home caused depression.

Interviewees also informed me that many Somali children and teenagers have untreated mental health issues resulting from trauma and stress relating to conflict, displacement, poverty, and poor adjustment. Asad has led several mental health literacy programs aimed at addressing mental health among Somali children and youth. "So far, we've met with several school principals, parents, local health-care providers, and the most active members of the Somali community. Our aim is to work with the children diagnosed with mental illness. We explain to Somali parents about what we do and clarify cultural myths surrounding mental illness."

Many possible myths lead patients not to seek treatment. Some Somalis may think patients are more violent than other people. Many assume mental illness is a Western phenomenon. "Back home, we never heard anything related to schizophrenia, bipolar disorder, stress, depression, anxiety disorders, eating disorders, mood disorders, or personality disorders. We called a crazy person the one who rips his clothes off and walks around naked. A crazy person was someone who harms himself or people around him,"[18] said

Mohamed. Another common myth is that there are no effective treatments for mental illness. Some Somali community members I spoke with argued that taking Western antidepressants would make the person more susceptible to severe depression and might increase the risk of suicide. According to nurses, many Somali patients avoid telling their doctors about their symptoms of depression because they're afraid they'll be prescribed antidepressants. Some may be afraid their neighbors will learn about them taking medication. This fear of antidepressants leads many to shun all types of treatments.

One interviewee recounted:

When my dad's doctor recommended antidepressant pills, our family sat to talk about whether or not he would take them as prescribed. We heard drugs used to treat depression often have undesirable side effects. I don't want to see my dad get worse and locked up in a mental institution. I don't want my dad to get tagged as a psychiatric patient in the end. My dad chose some alternative nondrug treatments such as meditation and faith healing.[19]

Apart from these myths, existing stigma within the community continues to be one of the major obstacles for individuals with mental illness. "Because of such stigma, a patient with mental illness may not seek advice from mental health professionals. Instead, they turn to spiritual healers, traditional practitioners, and herbalists," said one nurse. Other patients may be flown back home to seek alternative medicine not available in the Unites States, such as exorcism. This is one of the most commonly used techniques in Somalia to treat patients with a psychiatric disorder.

"Somali patients claim they suffer from some malevolent demons or spirits assumed to possess individuals," said Asad. "Some of these are known as *Zar, Mingis, Borama, Wadaado,* and many other maladies that are unknown to the Western world." Treatment for all these spirits depends on religious and traditional Somali healers. A community member who witnessed an exorcism ceremony conducted in Somalia explained:

Let me start with definitions of some of these *jinn* possessions. First, *Mingis* is a type of a spirit that primarily befalls more women than men. Secondly, *Zar* is a malevolent spirit possession that causes psychological discomfort or ailment, and thirdly, *Borama* is another type of unknown spirit possession cult that takes control of a human body. Because of these different types of demons, Somali people fall ill, so ceremonies are held in order to expel or appease the possessions that have detrimental effects to host. For most Somali patients, ailments and illnesses are ascribed to abstract beings. Because of such beliefs, several competing traditional shamans who deal with mental illness exist underground in some parts of the US. Some heal their clients through faith healing. These Muslim faith healing groups have their own exorcism retreats where they receive a large number of patients. During the exorcism procedure, the faith healers recite some specific verses of Quran over the purported patient. Some oracles claim they have the psychic aptitude to cure mental and physical illness through direct communication with the spirit world. Some others exorcise their clients by asking them to bathe in animal blood and then drink animal blood. They slaughter a ram as a sacrifice to the invasive spirits. Some dance around the patient while pleading the spirit to leave from the person peacefully. During exorcism, some patients enter a trance state. As soon as they regain consciousness, they claim they are already feeling better. The healing congregations involve a lavish feast, incantations, and musical performances.[20]

While interviewing Somalis, I found that women were more susceptible than their male counterparts to seek treatment from healers. "I kept in touch with faith healers who recited Quranic exorcism verses over me," one woman said. "These verses are believed to banish demons and heal illness. Before that, I went to an exorcist who held a ceremony to appease the evil supernatural being known as a jinn.[21] I came back looking in good physical and mental shape." Faith healers recommend their patients drink holy water known in Somalia as a *Tahliil*. The patient is encouraged to drink the sanctified water and sprinkle it on the body. Some faith healers advise their patients to wash their body with holy water over which the Quran has been recited. There are a few traditional healers who claim jinn cannot be expelled from the victim's body, and therefore, they consult with the unseen spirits. This group holds a ceremony to appease the jinn. Sacrifice, amulets, incantations, and the drinking of sheep's blood are integral parts of the jinn exorcism. No matter which healing methods traditional/faith healers use to treat their patients, their main healing objective is to remove the curse or cast out the spirit.

Apart from the stigma, Somali people also consider mental illness as abnormal, contagious, shameful, or a genetic disorder. One interviewee said, "Even today in the Somali community, calling someone crazy is offensive or demeaning." When one patient suffers from mental pain, the community may regard the patient's entire family unmarriageable. The actions or illness of one person can bring dishonor to the entire family unit.

Most Saint Cloud Somali community members attribute mental illness to the patient's spiritual deficiency. An Islamic religious scholar who prefers to remain anonymous said regular praying, meditation, and Quranic recitation will prevent a person from developing mental illness. This is a reason why individuals suffering mental health problems choose faith healers over psychologists and psychiatrists. Some patients consider seeing a mental health provider as a waste of time because they argue that only God can heal them.

To address Somali health problems, it is important to raise awareness and educate the community about the existing stigma toward mental illnesses. School-based mental health programs, if implemented, should create a welcoming environment specifically for Somali children who suffer from mental illnesses. Asad said he is willing to expand his services for children diagnosed with mental troubles. "I contacted Saint Cloud principals and explained to them that I set up a mental health program for schools that teaches coping mechanisms and getting rid of the stigma people associate with mental health problems. By doing so, these school-based mental health programs would include parents or family members. Recover Health Resources offers college and university student internships."[22]

Based on my interviews conducted for this book, I believe undiagnosed mental illness is very common in the community. As a Somali proverb goes, "*Waxaad qarsataa way ku qarsadaan,*" which literally means, *Whatever you hide, hides you.* It is important to destigmatize and normalize mental ailment because it is operating in the greater community every day. When we realize that mental health is not isolated to one particular ethnic, cultural, or religious group, we will break down the existing fear and shame surrounding the subject of mental illness. Therefore, cultural adaptation and competency are critically important for Somalis. The Somali community needs to adapt to the greater Saint Cloud / central Minnesota community and understand the American medical system without fear of losing the core essence of their culture. One Somali nurse told me it would be nice if local mental health providers and imams worked together. "I am not opposed to the Islamic faith healing at all," said the nurse. "I believe our local imams and religious scholars can remove the stigma surrounding mental illness."

For over two decades, the Somali community faced one of the most agonizing conflict experiences, followed by resettlement and problems with adjustment in their new country. These experiences have negatively impacted their general mental health. Lack of bilingual and bicultural mental health providers and services compatible with Somali culture may have constrained treatment of mental illness in the community. Asad said:

> Even though it is considered shameful to talk about emotional problems with people outside of the family, we encourage the community to learn the importance of an early intervention and prevention. Today, we see a lot of patients who are willing to seek treatment and counseling. My center is working very hard to raise awareness among the Somali community about mental health issues and ways to access treatment. We encourage the public not to isolate their family members who suffer from mental illness. We also hold group therapy sessions. The main objective of these sessions is to alleviate the stigma associated with mental health treatment.[23]

Transportation

The city has many Metro buses traveling back and forth on many routes, but older Somali people told me they faced three challenges in riding public transportation: they do not know their bus routes and surroundings well; they have no English skills to communicate with others if they get lost; they have financial difficulties. These barriers impact their ability to travel freely. "My dad gets on any bus he sees on the road," said Asho Hussein, whose father has gotten lost several times. "He has a hard time matching his route number to the route number on the bus. I came up with another technique that helps him not to get lost on his way back home. I wrote down our home address and destination stop on a piece of paper. Now he shows it to the driver when he gets on the bus."

Apart from the language and cultural barriers, transportation to and from the hospital is another challenge for new immigrants, especially the elderly. Even though there are agencies that provide transport to medical appointments, many health professionals informed me that Somalis, particularly those new to Saint Cloud, skip their medical appointments due to lack of transportation. This habit of not showing up frustrates many of the medical staff. "Most Somali seniors do not get on public transportation," said Abdirizak, a patient care extender. "They ask someone else they know to help take them to and from hospitals, or go with them just to act as transportation assistants." Most new Somali residents say that they depend on family and friends for transportation.

Most older Somalis are unaware of services available at Metro Bus. According to Debbie Anderson, community outreach / mobility manager:

> We offer a free travel training program here at Metro Bus. For those who are non-English speaking, we have two Somali travel trainers to meet with them. The training is designed to meet the needs of the rider; for some, they participate in multiple trainings until they are comfortable with riding the bus. During training, an individual will learn how to plan their trip, read schedules, pay their fare, and navigate the system. We found riding the bus for the first time was the biggest barrier to riding. We have many strong relationships within our community, with the support staff and services who work with the newly arrived refugees and immigrants. Often their staff refers individuals to our travel training program. Also, we have a Somali voice mail set up for individuals to call and request assistance with riding the bus. A travel trainer will return their call within forty-eight hours. We provide translated written materials as a resource. Seniors sixty-five and older can ride our fixed route bus at a reduced fare during non-peak hours. If an individual is not

able to navigate the fixed route bus because of a disability, we have our paratransit service. This service is door-to-door and translation is provided as part of the application process.[24]

Constant Mobility

Most Somalis move frequently as they look for better working opportunities. This frequent movement, with address changes, makes it difficult for health professionals to track their patients' prior medical history. Six in ten Somali refugees I spoke with had visited multiple health professionals within a year.

Conclusion

Most would agree that it's important to manage Somali patient relationships, caring for patients and working with their families to encourage preventive medical practices, following treatment plans correctly, and keeping emergency room visits to a minimum. To help health-care professionals close the cultural gap, hospitals and clinics should diversify their workplaces to facilitate better communication. They should hire bilingual and bicultural Somali nurses and public health officials who are willing to encourage culturally and religiously appropriate care, and educate the clinicians as well as the Somali community. After all, Somali patients with limited English have the right to the same level of medical attention as their English-speaking counterparts. Culturally and linguistically competent health-care services for Somalis will improve patient satisfaction, promote better understanding, and create mutual trust between health-care workers and their Somali patients.

Moreover, health-care providers should understand their patients deeply entrenched cultural beliefs and practices about the origin and prevention of illnesses. Without comprehension of their Somali patients' culture and values, the ability of health-care workers to build relationships with their Somali patients will be minimal. Thus, to provide effective care to patients from the Somali community, patient-provider communication is a decisive factor. Somali patients can best develop positive and trusting relationships when providers speak their language and understand their cultural traditions. Immigrants' sole dependency on emergency room use can only be reduced when patients develop the habit of contacting their personal health-care practitioners and physicians.

Health-care providers offer patients access to affordable and accessible care that will encourage them to seek preventive care before they end up in emergency rooms. When Somali Americans are taught the importance of preventive care, they can avoid unnecessary and ultimately more costly hospital admissions. This chapter shows the factors hampering the delivery of proper health care and the need to make Somalis aware of alternative transportation options for trips to medical clinics.

Conclusion

IN THIS BOOK, I HAVE USED INTERVIEWS with Somali members of the Saint Cloud community to explain their lives, culture, views on issues of integration and assimilation, challenges facing their businesses, and the health care issues they deal with.

Somalis in Saint Cloud want to integrate into the broader community and be both Somali and American. We see traces of Somali integration everywhere—students in the schools, shoppers in the stores, and workers in our businesses; Somalis are fully engaged members of the Saint Cloud community and have no desire to be an isolated enclave. However, like many ethnic Americans, Somalis do not want to assimilate to the extent of losing important parts of their culture, religious beliefs, and practices. Like many other ethnic minorities, Somalis believe in a diverse, pluralistic "salad bowl" America in which one keeps one's ethnic and religious identity and combines it with an identity of American citizenship and patriotism.

There were no substantial numbers of Somali businesses to speak of in the Saint Cloud area in the year 2000. Today, the Somali community is growing and so are their businesses. Somalis own restaurants, coffee shops, clothing and grocery stores, taxi and truck transportation services, travel agencies, automobile insurance companies, tax return services, and so on. These family-owned businesses offer employment opportunities for Somalis and cater to their ethnic clients. Some new businesses have started providing services to Somalis and non-Somalis alike. For many small-business owners, becoming their own boss is the main thing that encourages them to set up their own companies.

Somali business boosts Saint Cloud's economic growth, employment rates, and community development, yet small-business owners face obstacles that may restrict their businesses. Those salient challenges include language and cultural barriers, a lack of credit history, access to capital, investment partnerships, and access to business networks. Other issues include restrictions on loan-taking due to the Islamic religion, market saturation, and a lack of a friendly environment conducive for business expansion.

In 2015, I joined the Saint Cloud Area Chamber of Commerce Diversity Council; its mission is to advocate, enhance, and promote equality of opportunity for all businesses.[1] What the Chamber has done is a good start, and I expect other organizations to come up with inclusivity and diversity plans. Such efforts will help Somali-owned businesses learn how to develop business plans, expand their clientele, and capitalize on better networking opportunities.

Somalis in central Minnesota not only face obstacles in the formation and expansion of family-owned businesses but also in health care. Despite a growing Somali population in Saint Cloud, some American health providers seem to have a hard time understanding the Somali cultural approach to medical care. Delivering care to Somali patients depends on a rudimentary understanding of their medical and health beliefs and practices. Somalis came to central Minnesota with customs, rituals, and health-care beliefs and practices unique to them. These practices are alien to the host community's physicians. When Somalis arrived in the United States, they found American medical practices very different from what they knew back home in Somalia. Some of the greatest hurdles to good health care facing Somalis include their inadequate health literacy, religious and cultural practices, and limited English skills.

To better serve Somalis, health-care providers should understand their patients' deeply ingrained cultural beliefs, practices, and feelings about the prevention of diseases. Health-care workers must build relationships with their Somali patients. I understand how important it is to have good patient-provider communication. At the same time, Somali patients need to develop positive and trusting relationships with their physicians and nurses. Somalis' reliance on emergency room care can be reduced when health-care providers offer Somalis access to affordable and accessible care, which will encourage them to seek preventive care before they end up in emergency rooms, paying for unnecessary and costly hospital admissions.

These are important points that I hope readers and will take from this study. Addressing these issues will benefit the entire Saint Cloud community.

Postscript

If people come together, they can
even mend a crack in the sky.

—Somali proverb

THE TRAGIC EVENTS OF SEPTEMBER 17, 2016, took place after all the interviews for this book were completed. That night, while driving back from Minneapolis, one of my close friends called me and told me a man randomly stabbed several people at the Saint Cloud Crossroads Center mall with a knife. As soon as I heard, I froze. I frequently shop at the mall, and I know some friends who work there. I called my brother who worked at a store nearby the mall. He did not answer his phone. Then I started worrying about him.

I immediately prayed that nothing bad had happened to my brother and friends. Getting back to Saint Cloud took longer than expected that night.

I drove to the mall and stood with community members in the Target parking lot. One of the community elders said the attacker was a Somali American man. I froze in fear, sweaty and with my mouth wide open. I never thought something like this would take place in our city.

This event shocked and disturbed everyone in Saint Cloud, including members of the Somali community. Somalis' hearts went out to the victims of this type of violence, from which they themselves had fled in Somalia. Somalis stood with the Saint Cloud community in the face of the tragedy and came together. Hundreds of students from the local colleges and universities took to the streets to show unity in diversity, chanting the slogan, "We are one and united."

Somali and non-Somali leaders congregated at City Hall to call for solidarity and harmony after the stabbings. While there, I met some of the top Somali and host community leaders in the Saint Cloud area. We discussed how best we could come out unified. Deep down, I knew fear and suspicion would not make us divided. So, we chose to join hands. After the incident, nonprofit groups and faith leaders did a remarkable job organizing to heal the pain and restore relationships. English-, Spanish-, and Somali-speaking communities in the city of Saint Cloud organized a peace walk on October 10, 2016, chanting, "Unity, midnimo, and unidos." The peace rally energized our solidarity and our belief that we could set aside our own fears and build a cohesive community, free from mistrust, hatred, and stereotypes.

The *Social Capital Survey: Central Minnesota* showed that trust in Somalis went up from 56 percent in 2010 to 73 percent in 2015. With efforts like those mentioned above, I'm hopeful that this growing level of trust has not been negatively impacted by the tragedy, but we must always build and rebuild relationships and trust.

Saint Cloud Mayor Dave Kleis and Saint Cloud police chief Blair Anderson did a great job assuring the public that the city would recuperate, and they focused on standing together. "The city will remain vigilant and resolved to not compromise in building community. We're not going to change our course of what this community is founded upon and this nation is founded upon. We need to stand together as a community. That bedrock and foundation, although shaken, will not be taken off that foundation," Mayor Kleis told the press.[2]

The 2016 election, in which political candidates were elected to office after saying negative, frightening things about Muslims and Somalis, created some fear and suspicion within the Somali community. One thing is for certain: the need for better understanding and connection is even greater now. However, I don't think the Crossroads Center event has changed Somali perspectives and practices regarding integration and assimilation or the challenges facing Somali businesses and health care, major topics I covered in this book.

What can be done to continue building an inclusive Saint Cloud community? I would like to provide one good example: the programs piloted by the Central Minnesota Community Empowerment Organization (CMCEO). I know these programs well because I am a board member of CMCEO. One program is Take Ten, which teaches youth at Apollo and Tech High Schools interpersonal and conflict resolution skills; it received a Saint Cloud School District 742 Partners in Education Award in May 2016. I teach a Take Ten class at Tech High School. CMCEO members have also helped facilitate Circles of Understanding, in which diverse members of the Saint Cloud community get to know each other. These programs help us all better understand each other and strengthen relationships in our community. Dr. Ron Pagnucco, a Peace Studies professor at the College of Saint Benedict and chair of the CMCEO board, summarized these programs; I will quote him here:

> The Central Minnesota Community Empowerment Organization (CMCEO) works largely with the Somali community in the Saint Cloud area. CMCEO has several projects, including Take Ten, a curriculum developed at the University of Notre Dame in collaboration with their community partner, the Robinson Community Learning Center. The curriculum focuses on interpersonal social and conflict resolution skills and is taught by diverse teams of trained college students to diverse classes of high school students. The Take Ten project received a District 742 Partners in Education Award in spring 2016. We also have a Get to Work program, which helps applicants locate jobs, fill out applications, and prepare for jobs, and follows up after the applicant gets the job. Jobs are critically important for the well-being and integration of refugees and immigrants. The program helped 124 refugees and immigrants get jobs over the past couple of years. Our Community Education program successfully concluded its fall 2016 Conversational Somali and Introduction to Somali Culture course.

Based on the positive feedback of the participants, we will offer a course on the "Lives and Culture of Somalis in Saint Cloud" in the spring of 2017. Clearly, there is an interest in learning about our Somali neighbors, and we hope to have members of the broader community join Somali participants so we also can have dialogue on the issues facing Saint Cloud. We collaborate with Ms. Hudda Ibrahim's Emerging Somali Women Leaders group, which is doing a very good job because of Hudda's truly empowering mentorship. CMCEO also helps with tutoring Somali students because we believe education is essential for advancement, and we are planning Circles of Understanding that bring together diverse members of the community using the circles process to help build relationships, to discuss issues and plan action. In collaboration with the Peace Studies Department at Saint John's / Saint Ben's, we continue to explore ways to build a stronger community and address conflicts and challenges.

I strongly believe building relationships and developing trust are crucial at this juncture. I hope you will join the effort.

Glossary of Key Non-English Terms

ONLY KEY TERMS FREQUENTLY USED IN the text are listed here. The terms below may have multiple spellings depending on the variation of Somali regions and clans. In my book, I used anglicized spellings to help non-Somali readers pronounce them.

Abaya: [App a yuh] A loose black robe that is traditionally worn by Muslim women from head to toe

Aday: [Add day] A chewing stick for a toothbrush

Aslama: [Az lamma] To surrender

Ayuuto: [A you toh] A community-based form of microfinancing; a group of women contributes an equal amount of money to their group and one person takes the donated pool at a time.

Darod: [Duh rod] One of the major Somali clans

Dugsi: [Dughzy] A Quranic school

Eid al-Adha: [Eid ul- ad huh] Feast of Sacrifice

Eid al-Fitr: [Eid ul fiter] Festival that marks the end of the fasting month of Ramadan

Fajr: [Fuh jar] Sunrise prayer

Guur: [Gour] Marriage; the root word is derived from *Guurid*, meaning to move one location to another

Hadith: [Ha-deeth] A tradition that is based on the sayings and activities of Prophet Mohammed and his companions

Hajj: [Hatch] The fifth pillar of Islam is a pilgrimage to Mecca, the birthplace of Mohammed and the holiest city of Islam; a Muslim is expected to make a religious journey to Mecca at least once in a lifetime

Halal: [Hal lull] Permissible by Islamic law

Hawiye: [Ha wee yeh] One of the major Somali clans

Hijab: [He-jab] The custom of some women dressing modestly outside the home

Hus: [Huse] Anniversary celebration of a loved one's passing

Iddah: [E-duh] A period of waiting when a widow may not marry another man

Imam: [E-mom] The man who leads prayers in a mosque

Injera: [Ein-cheeruh] The Ethiopian tangy and spongy flatbread

Islam: [Iz lam] Submission to the will of God

Jahannam: [Ja-huh-nam] A place of eternal fire intended as punishment for the damned; also the abode of Satan and the forces of evil where sinners suffer eternal punishment

Janna: [Jannah] The abode of righteous souls after death

Jilbab: [Jeel-bob] A type of a loose veil

Jinn: [Djinn] Demon; an invisible spirit that appears in the form of humans or animals that is mentioned in the Quran and believed by Muslims to inhabit the people and influence their behavior

Madrasa: [Ma daruhza] A Quranic school; an Islamic religious school where the children learn how to memorize the Quran

Maghrib: [Mug rib] Sunset prayer

Malawah: [Mal-wuh] Crepes

Miswak: [Miss wak] A chewing stick for a tooth-
              brush

Mohammed: [Moha med] (Some people spell it as
              Muhammed or Mohammad.) A Muslim
              prophet who, according to Islam, was the
              last messenger of Allah

Quran: [Ko ran] (Some people spell it as Quran,
              Qur'an, or Koran.) Islam's revealed scrip-
              ture; Islamic Holy Book, given by Allah to
              the Prophet

Ramadan: [Ram ah dawn] The ninth month of the
              Islamic calendar; the month of fasting; the
              holiest period for the Islamic faith

Sab: [Sap] A collection of clan families [the Ra-
              hanwein and the Digil] that inhabit south-
              ern Somalia

Sahan: [Sa' hun] Pioneer

Salaam: [Sal lam] Peace

Salah: [sal luh] A prayer (Fajr, the early-morning
              prayer performed before sunrise, 4:00 to
              6:00 a.m.; Duhr, the midday prayer per-
              formed between 12:00 and 1:00 p.m.; Asr,
              the late-afternoon prayer performed from
              3:00 to 5:00 p.m.; Maghrib, the sunset
              prayer performed immediately after the

sun sets; and Isha, the night prayer. It is preferable to pray Isha before midnight.)

Salat al-Janazah: [Salad-tool- jeenuhzuh] The Islamic funeral prayer where Muslims ask God to pardon the sins of the deceased; performed in congregation at the mosque before the body is transported to the grave

Salatul Jumu'ah: [Salad-tool- joomah] Special Friday congregational prayer

Samaale: [Sam aleh] A collection of major Somali clan families that inhabit the south, central, and northern regions of Somalia

Sawm: [Saum] (Some people spell it as Sawn.) Fasting in the month of Ramadan; the fasting often falls in either June, July, or August

Sharia: [Cha ree-ah] The law of Islam mainly derived from the Quran and from the teachings and example of Prophet Mohammed

Sheikh: [Sheik] Title given to a Muslim scholar/ leader

Soomaal: [So- mal] Means, *Go and milk for yourself;* illustrates the generosity and hospitality of the Somali pastoral nomads when they offer a traveling guest fresh milk

Sunni: [Sunny] One of the two main branches of orthodox Islam

Tahliil: [Tah leal] Holy water that has been blessed by a pious person for use in treatment for ailments and prevention of the evil eye

Takbir: [Tak beer] Proclamation of the God's greatness, such as reciting the phrase "God is great"

Taraweeh: [Tara- weeh] A special nighttime prayer performed in congregation

Tayammum: [Tayah-mum] The use of dry ablution that is alternative to ritual washing

Wanqal: [One cull] The slaughtering of a male sheep for a banquet to seek a blessing for the newborn baby

Welwel: [Well well] Stress

Wudu: [Wo-dooh] The ritual washing of hands before performing prayer

Zakat: [Zah-cat] The fourth pillar of Islam is almsgiving; this practice is equivalent to an act of worship

For Further Reading

Abdullahi, Mohamed Diriye. *Culture and Customs of Somalia.* Westport, CN: Greenwood Press, 2001.

Elmi, Afyare Abdi. *Understanding the Somalia Conflagration: Identity, Political Islam and Peacebuilding.* London: Pluto Press, 2010.

Lewis, I. M. *A Modern History of the Somali: Nation and State in the Horn of Africa.* Oxford: James Currey, 2002.

Metz, Helen Chapin. *Somalia: A Country Study.* Washington, D.C.: Federal Research Division, 1992.

Endnotes

CHAPTER 1

1   Afyare Abdi Elmi, *Understanding the Somalia Conflagration: Identity, Political Islam, and Peacebuilding* (London: Pluto Press, 2010), 48.

2   I. M. Lewis, *A Modern History of the Somali: Nation and State in the Horn of Africa* (Oxford: James Currey, 2002), 1.

3   Helen Chapin Metz, *Somalia: A Country Study* (Washington, D.C.: Federal Research Division, 1992), xxi.

4   Elmi, *Understanding the Somalia Conflagration*, 30.

5   The community elder was an ex-Somali military leader during the conflict between Somalia and Ethiopia who refused to have his name mentioned in this book.

CHAPTER 2

1   Hudda Ibrahim, *The Traveler*, unpublished memoir.

2   UN High Commissioner for Refugees website, "What is a Refugee" www.unrefugees.org/what-is-a refugee/; see also 1951 UN Refugee Convention and 1967 Refugee Convention Protocol.

3   John F. Kennedy, *A Nation of Immigrants* (New York: Anti-Defamation League, 1958).

4   Anne Gillespie Lewis, *Swedes in Minnesota* (Saint Paul: Minnesota Historical Society Press, 2004), 5.

5   Jon Gjerde and Carlton C. Qualey, *Norwegians in Minnesota* (Saint Paul: Minnesota Historical Society Press, 2002), 1.

6   King Banaian and Mónica García-Perez, "St. Cloud Immigration: A Fact Sheet—A Review of Census data," School of Public Affairs Research Institute.

7   US Census Bureau, *The Foreign-Born Population: 2000* (Washington, D.C.: US Census Bureau, 2003).

8   Allison Liuzzi, *Immigration in Minnesota: A Changing Story*, Minnesota Compass, May 2006, http://www.mncompass.org/immigration/overview.

9   Diana Briton Putman and Mohamood Cabdi Noor, *The Somalis: Their History and Culture* (Washington, D.C.: Refugee Service Center, Center for Applied Linguistics, 1993.)

10   Mark Bradbury and Sally Healy, *Whose Peace Is It Anyway? Connecting Somali and International Peacemaking* (London: Conciliation Resources, 2010), 10.

11   Hussein Mohamud lived in a Dadaab refugee camp in northeastern Kenya for many years. Hussein came to Tennessee in 2013. After living in Tennessee, he moved to Saint Cloud to join his sister. Now he goes to St. Cloud Community College and works at hospitals as an interpreter. He is a refugee advocate in Saint Cloud, Minnesota.

12   Ali Abdulle

13   Ibrahim, *The Traveler.*

14   Abdi Mahad, a research analyst; Abdi wrote several articles about Somali culture.

15   USCIS, *Applicant Performance on the Naturalization Test*, May 2016, https://www.uscis.gov/us-citizenship/naturalization-test/applicant-performance-naturalization-test.

16   Mohamed Abdullahi, a father whose children live in Africa, talks about the importance of being a US citizen; he travels back and forth to visit his family.

17   Hussein Mohamud

18   Abdi Mahad

19   Hussein Mohamud

20   Abdi Hassan was among the first Somali immigrants who came to Saint Cloud to explore job opportunities in the area. I met him at Caribou Coffee on Tuesday, August 30, 2016.

21   Mohamoud Mohamed, executive director of the Saint Cloud Somali Salvation Organization, known as SASSO. SASSO was the first Somali American organization established in Saint Cloud.

22   "An Initiative Foundation," *IQ*, Spring 2004,15.

23   Mohamoud Mohamed, Abdi Hassan, and six others told me the Somalis
        moved from Marshall to Saint Cloud.

24   Minnesota Department of Human Services, *Refugees Arrived in Minnesota
        from Overseas—By Country of Origin, 01/01/2015 – 12/31/2015.*

25   Mohamoud Mohamed, the executive director of the Saint Cloud Area
        Somali Salvation Organization

26   Mohamoud Mohamed

27   Abdi Hassan

28   Abdirahman Nur, June 16, 2016

29   Mohamud Mohamed

30   Ali Abdi's family moved from Mayfield, Kentucky, in 2013.

31   Fathiya Mohamed, refugee program supervisor at Lutheran Social
        Services

32   Fathiya Mohamed

33   Mohamed Ismael moved to Saint Cloud from Arizona.

34   Nejah Ibrahim, August 14, 2016, Saint Cloud

35   Abdi Hassan

36   Mohammed Abdi moved with his family to Saint Cloud in 2014. He
        originally was resettled in Nebraska. After a brief stay, he decided to join
        his immediate relatives living in Minnesota.

CHAPTER 3

1   Ali Osman, Saint Cloud, April 11, 2016

2   Abdi Mahad

3   Abdi Mahad

4   Abdi Mahad

5   Abdi Mahad

6   Abdi Mahad

7   Abdi Mahad; I was fifteen years old when a woman in our apartment building
      asked me to perform a naming ritual for her child. For the first time, I did not
      know what the *Gordaadin* ritual meant. My mom explained it to me well. Mothers
      expected their babies to treasure education like the way I did when I was a child.

8   William Conton, *The African* (London: Heinemann, 1966), 21.

9   Saeed believes that immigration caused most Somali children to be disrespectful of their parents' orders.

10   Abdi Mahad

11   Abdi Mahad explains about the formation of clan systems in Somali community.

12   The lunar calendar used by Muslims, consisting of twelve months of twenty-nine or thirty days each, totaling 353 or 354 days. Each month begins at the sighting of a new moon.

13   Abdi Mahad teaches Somali language to Native American professionals and professors in Saint Cloud twice a week for an hour.

14   Abdi Mahad

15   Basheer Mohamed, "A New Estimate of the US Muslim Population," January 6, 2016, http://www.pewresearch.org/fact-tank/2016/01/06/a-new-estimate-of-the-u-s-muslim-population.

16   An instructor who teaches Quran memorization for the children born in the United States

17   Sheikh Hassan, on April 18, 2016 at Mogadishu Mall

18   The imam of the mosque

19   Afyare Abdi Elmi, *Understanding the Somalia Conflagration: Identity, Political Islam, and Peacebuilding* (London: Pluto Press, 2010), 48.

20   I. M. Lewis, *Understanding Somalia and Somaliland: Culture, History, Society* (New York: Columbia University Press, 2008).

21   Sheikh Hassan, the imam of the Saint Cloud mosque

22   Sheikh Hassan

23   Wahhabis consider themselves puritans and reformers. The founder, Mohammed Bin Abdul Wahhab (1703–1787), wanted to see caliphates ruling the Muslim world. In the 1970s, many young Somalis traveled to the Gulf countries to work and pursue Islamic education. After having completed their education, students returned home with an extreme ideology different from what Somalis used to embrace for centuries. Somali people predominantly followed Sufism, Islamic mysticism. Sufi followers challenged the rise of new scholars spreading extreme interpretations of Islam. During the conflict years in 1991, the Islamist groups took arms and formed alliances to propagate their thinking throughout Somalia.

CHAPTER 4

1   See J. F. Dovidio, S. L. Gaertner, A. R. Pearson, and B. M. Riek, "Social identities and Social Context: Social Attitudes and Personal Well-Being," *Social Identities in Groups: Advances in Group Processes*, vol. 22 (2005), 231–260; A. Ager and A. Strang, "Understanding Integration: A Conceptual Framework," *Journal of Refugees Studies* 21, no. 2 (2008): 166–190; Richard T. Schaeffer, *Racial and Ethnic Groups* (Upper Saddle River, NJ: Pearson Education, 2011), 24.

2   Ibid.

3   Schaeffer, *Racial and Ethnic Groups*, 23.

4   Ibid.

5   Abdi Mahad

6   Abdi Mahad

7   Ahmed Ali

8   Abdi Mahad

9   Abdi Mahad

10   Ahmed Ali, a lead organizer at the Greater Minnesota Worker Center, Saint Cloud, June 16, 2016

11   Abdirizak Jama, twenty-two-years old, a patient care extender, Saint Cloud, June 16, 2016

12   Abdi Mahad, July 16, 2016

13   Abdirahim Osman, a businessman

14   Abdi Daisane works at Resource Inc. Employment Action Center.

15   Jenny Berg, "Trust of Minorities, Other Area People up Since 2010," February 26, 2016, *Saint Cloud Times*, http://www.sctimes.com/story/news/local/2016/02/26/trust-minorities-other-area-people-up-since-2010/80924242/.

16   Ahmed Ali

17   Liuzzi, *Immigration in Minnesota*.

18   Kristi Marohn, "Fact Check: Somali Student Numbers," *Saint Cloud Times*, January 24, 2016, http://www.sctimes.com/story/news/local/immigration/2016/01/24/fact-check-somali-student-numbers/79062702/.

19   Abdirizak Jama

20   Abdi Daisane ran for Saint Cloud City Council in 2015. Even though
      he did not win, his effort will encourage other younger Somalis to get
      involved in in their city of Saint Cloud.

21   Abdi Mahad

22   Omar Podi

23   Omar Podi

CHAPTER 5

1   Tohow Siad

2   Tohow Siad

3   Mohamed Beene-Beene, executive director of the Minnesota Somali
      Chamber of Commerce

4   Tarabi Jama, executive director of Gateway, August 19, 2016, Saint
      Cloud, Minnesota

5   Farah Guled, manager of the Mogadishu restaurant

6   Tarabi Jama

7   Farah Guled

8   Tarabi Jama

9   Mohammed Yusuf, owner of Kaah Express

10   Tohow Siad

11   Tarabi Jama, executive director of Gateway, August 19, 2016, Saint
      Cloud, Minnesota

12   Abdi Mahad

13   Zeinab Mohamed, the owner of the Zeinab Clothing Store at
      Mogadishu Business Premise

14   Shamhad

CHAPTER 6

1   *Merriam-Webster Dictionary*

2   Ismael Khalif, the owner of Afya Pharmacy. Ismael came to the United
      States in 2000. He went to Texas. He moved to Minneapolis in 2013 and
      found a job at Walgreens. While he was working as a pharmacy technician,

the idea of setting a new pharmacy in Somali-populated cities was born. He visited Saint Cloud and Rochester four times to assess the possibility of starting up a pharmacy. During his visit, he discerned a huge gap in the medical and health-care system for the Somali community with limited English proficiency in central Minnesota. After meticulously planning his market niche, he eventually opened his pharmacy in Saint Cloud at 3407 Third St. N. in March 2015. He caters to Somali customers.

3   A nurse who didn't want to have her name mentioned in this book

4   A Somali man who asked me not to mention his name

5   Stephanie Dickrell, "CentraCare Hopes to Close Cultural Gap in Diabetes Care," *Saint Cloud Times*, May 20, 2015, http://www.sctimes.com/story/news/local/2015/05/19/centracare-hopes-close-cultural-gap-diabetes-care/27591017/.

6   Sadman Rahman, "Profs Help Somali Kids with Diabetes," *Minnesota Daily*, September 14, 2015, http://www.mndaily.com/article/2015/09/profs-help-somali-kids-diabetes.

7   CentraCare, "CentraCare Health Receives Grant to Improve Diabetes Care for Diverse Patients," April 23, 2015, https://www.centracare.com/about-us/news-publications/news/2015/grant-to-improve-diabetes-care-for-diverse-patients/.

8   Fathiya Mohamed

9   Abdirizak, a patient care extender

10   US Census Bureau, *American Community Survey Reports: Language Use in the United States: 2007*, accessed June 18, 2010, http://www.census.gov/prod/2010pubs/acs-12.pdf.

11   Ali Mohamud, an old patient who claims that anyone who has been in the United States long enough can become an interpreter

12   Ahmed, Ali Mohamud's son, who feels doctors do not want him to interpret for his father, a stroke patient

13   Zeinab Abdi, sixty-two-year-old mother who has no English skills, uses her daughter for all interpretation purposes.

14   Asad Mohamed, the executive director and founder of Recover Health Resources, August 30, 2016

15   Asad Mohamed

16   Asad Mohamed

17   Farhiya Idifle, a social worker

18   Asad Mohamed

19   An interviewee who refused to have his name mentioned in the book

20   The community member who witnessed such an exorcism in Somalia asked me not to mention his name in the book. He described more than I could write in this book.

21   *Jinn*—an invisible spirit that appears in the form of humans or animals. The jinn is mentioned in the Quran, and most Muslims believe that it inhabits the person and influences people's well-being.

22   Asad Mohamed

23   Asad Mohamed

24   Debbie Anderson, community outreach / mobility manager at Metro Bus, December 28, 2016

CONCLUSION

1   This is the mission of the Saint Cloud Area Chamber of Commerce Diversity Council. Now I am the vice chair of the Diversity Council.

2   Jenny Berg, "Kleis on Crossroads Attack: This Keeps Me Up at Night," *Saint Cloud Times*, September 18, 2016, http://www.sctimes.com/story/news/local/2016/09/18/kleis-crossroads-attack-keeps-me-up-night/90617354/.

About the Author

HUDDA IBRAHIM, MA, IS A FACULTY MEMBER at St. Cloud Technical and Community College, where she teaches diversity and social justice. Hudda specializes in international peace studies, conflict resolution, policy analysis, and political change. She sits on several nonprofit boards, including the Central Minnesota Community Empowerment Organization, United Way of Saint Cloud, Minnesota, and the Saint Cloud Area Chamber of Commerce, in which she is diversity council vice chair. She has published articles on reconciliation, mediation, the role of Somali traditional elders, and the use of customary law in Somalia. She has contributed articles to the *Huffington Post* and other news sources, both local and international.

Hudda's interests include conflict transformation, the politics of reconciliation, global politics, transitional justice, gender issues, and war and peace. She has given talks on issues of community relationship building, peace, human rights, women's empowerment and inclusion in politics, and alternative world futures at colleges, universities, churches, and other venues. She has written three other books: *The Traveler*, a memoir about her work, contributions, and life journey; *Get in the Driving Seat of Your Own Life: Steps to Unleash Women's Confidence*, a book that encourages girls and women to pursue their God-given potential and understand their abilities in order to flourish and be successful in the United States; and *The Role of the Traditional Somali Model in Peacemaking: Why Reconciliation Was Maintained in Somaliland but Disintegrated in the South of Somalia*, based on her MA thesis. She holds a master's degree in peace studies from the University of Notre Dame and a bachelor's degree in peace and conflict studies and English literature from the College of Saint Benedict and Saint John's University in Minnesota.

Hudda is the founder and president of Filsan Consultant LLC. Filsan works with local businesses and related entities to provide three revenue-generating services: consulting, speaking engagements, and training for the employer. Hudda is a change agent, providing necessary resources to bring the central Minnesota community and new American populations together. In doing so, businesses and community members can learn about each other and leverage their cultural backgrounds in innovative ways to create successful business relationships.

On weekends, Hudda mentors a cohort of young Somali women. She has strived to be known as an engaging and effective advocate for the educational and social needs of students and adults throughout an increasingly large and diverse community. In her spare time, she reads books and magazines.

In recognition of her leadership, Hudda has received numerous awards. These include the 5 under 40 Award, 2016 Difference Maker, 2016 Partners in Education District 742 Award for the Take Ten project, and the Women's Group project. The Somali American National Institute has offered her an appreciation award for her work in the community.